CW00547087

When Readin

Adrian Moulton was a special needs teacher for 40 years, teaching English, Drama and Music. A regular broadcaster on local radio, he still writes, records and performs with Reading's post-punk heroes The Complaints. Married, with children, stepchildren, grandchildren and great-grandchildren aplenty, he works in the Sound Machine in Reading.

Mike Warth was born and educated in Reading before completing teacher training at Milton Keynes College of Education. He taught in primary schools for 28 years, after which he was appointed as an Education Officer for Special Education, retiring in 2013. He is currently working part-time in the Sound Machine in Reading and is the author of two books on local history, as well as a significant contributor to a series of books on rock music. He is married with three children, one grandchild and two stepchildren.

Austin Matthews grew up in Crowthorne and moved to Reading after graduating from university some 20 (or so) years ago. By day he works in finance but by night picks up a pen to write about obscure progressive rock acts for various publications. Married with two children, he is still searching for an original copy of Grannie's self-titled album from 1971. If you have one, get in touch.

Also published by Two Rivers Press

When Reading Really Rocked

The Live Music Scene in Reading 1966–1976

Adrian Moulton, Mike Warth
& Austin Matthews

TWO
RIVERS
PRESS

First published in the UK in 2020 by Two Rivers Press
7 Denmark Road, Reading RG1 5PA
www.tworiverspress.com

ISBN 978-1-909747-65-4

3 4 5 6 7 8 9

Two Rivers Press is represented in the UK by Inpress Ltd
and distributed by NBNi.

Cover photograph by Adrian Moulton
Cover lettering by Sally Castle
Text and cover design by Nadja Guggi and typeset in Parisine

Printed and bound in Great Britain by TJ Books Limited, Padstow

Acknowledgements

Thanks to the following for their assistance:

Special thanks
Rob Callaghan for his excellent input on the sections about the Reading Festival. Rob relocated to Reading in 1987 because Luton never had an After Dark club. Having tormented Bedfordshire and North Hertfordshire in local DIY psych-punk band The Twitch, he half-heartedly tried a similar incursion in Berkshire but failed. He was successful as a music and club promoter in the 00s but now lives happily as a punter, occasionally poking a finger into a suitable musical pie.

Neal Turner and Steve Edwards of Sound Machine, Reading's finest record shop. They not only put up with Adrian and Mike nattering to potential customers about the book for hours, but also paid them for the privilege!

Interviews
Paul Alexander, Keith Allen, Les Calvert, Alan Clayson, Martin Cole, Mike Cooper, Richard Cox-Smith, Trevor Darks, Steve Eagles, John Elton, Stewart Harding, Gerald T. Moore, Richard Niles, Dave Plummer, Chris Smythe, John Stannard, Patrick Wass

Anecdotes, e-mails, pictures/illustrative material
Bob Ainsworth, John 'Olly' Alcock, Nick Allcock, Roger Austin, John Boman, Chris Braclik, Kelvin Bullen, James Carter, Annabel Chapman, Pete Choules, Charles Clark, Keith Clark, Dave Clifton, Tony Clixby, Hugh Crabtree, Sue Crook, Janet Davis, Colin Dixon, Ray Dorey, John Duncalfe, Kevin Dyson, Mike Eastman, Peter Excell, Gerry Field, Charles Frean, Peter Green, Janie Grote, Andrew Haig, Malcolm Hamerston, Graham Hames, Mike Harper, David Harrison, Don Heaton, Barry Hill, Steve & Fiona Holloway, Stuart Hopper, Peter Hughes, Paul Irwin, Alan Jacobs, Steve James, Geoff Lawrence, Steve Lusted, Alastair MacDonald, Paul Manning, Andy Martin,

Paul McColm, Matt Mead, Linda Metcalfe, Derek Miles, Mick New, Yvonne Nicholson, Eddie Page, Barry Painter, Henry Paulinsky, Colin Peake, Andy Pegg, Sylvia Peretz, Nigel Reveler, Eddie Richardson, Mike Sebbage, Mike Shonfield, Michael Simpson, John Tierney, Ian Tyler, Dave White, Paul Whiteway, Trevor Young

Staff at the following libraries
The University of Reading, Reading Technical College, Reading Local Studies Library, The British Library

Also
Marie Copley, Clare Matthews, Purco Print

Picure credits

While every effort has been made to trace the copyright holders and obtain permission to reproduce the photographs included in this book, we would like to apologise should there have been any errors or omissions. Please do get in touch with any enquiries or any information relating to images which we have been unable to credit.

7: © Terry Allsop; 8: Photo courtesy of Mike Cooper; 11: unknown photographer (ANEFO) CC0 1.0 (https://commons.wikimedia.org/wiki/File:GeorgieFame1966.jpg); 12 (Amboy Dukes): © Mirrorpix/Reach Licensing; 12: Photo courtesy of Les Calvert; 13: Photo courtesy of Mike Shonfield; 14: Photo courtesy of John Stannard; 16: Photo courtesy of Mike Shonfield; 22: *Shell*; 26: *Shell*; 27: © Terry Allsop; 34: *Shell*; 36: © Terry Allsop; 36: Courtesy of Martin Cole; 39: Courtesy of John Stannard; 40: © Terry Allsop; 42: *Shell*; 45: Photo courtesy of Les Calvert; 47: Dick Jordan, with kind permission of Peter Hughes; 49: *Shell*; 51: Courtesy of Mike Easterman; 53: Courtesy of Les Calvert; 54: Photo courtesy of Les Calvert; 55: *Shell*; 61: © Terry Allsop; 64: © Terry Allsop; 64: Courtesy of Patrick Wass; 65: Courtesy of Patrick Wass; 68: Courtesy of Les Calvert; 71: Courtesy of Paul Alexander 79: © Adrian Moulton; 84: Courtesy of Malcolm Hamerston; 91: Courtesy of John 'Olly' Alcock; 100: Courtesy of Les Calvert; 107: David Major CC BY 2.0 (https://commons.wikimedia.org/wiki/File:Reading_Festival_1975_(5).jpg); 108: David Major CC BY 2.0 (https://commons.wikimedia.org/wiki/File:Reading_Festival_1975_(11).jpg); 109: David Major CC BY 2.0 (https://commons.wikimedia.org/wiki/File:Reading_Festival_1975_(1).jpg); 114: David Major CC BY 2.0 "Reading Festival" (https://https://www.flickr.com/photos/deargdoom57/3388689294/in/set-72157617097683540/); 120: unknown photographer; 123: *Shell*; 126: Photo courtesy of Les Calvert; 129: Photo courtesy of Les Calvert; 133: Courtesy of Mike Warth.

Contents

Foreword

Robinson in Space, a 1997 film by Patrick Keiller, begins with a train leaving Paddington station heading for the narrator's first stop – Reading. As the train pulls out, he muses that

> 'Although I can see how beautiful anything could be, if only I could change it, in practically every case there is nothing I can really do. Everything is changed into something else in my imagination, then the dead weight of things changes it back into what it was in the first place. A bridge between imagination and reality must be built.'*

Reading in the 1960s was often thought of as a sleepy provincial town in the south of England too close to London for anything to really happen there. In retrospect this was far from true.

In 1958 when I left school there were two jazz clubs and at least three coffee houses where youth would gather, one of which was a very bohemian joint called the Jag Bar situated three floors up from the street on Jacksons Corner. A couple of years later there was the Latin Quarter on Bridge Street: a cellar bar where local groups played, a ground floor coffee house and an upstairs bar and another venue where on Sunday afternoons there was a jazz jam session open to all-comers. I played double bass for the first time in my life (and probably the last) during one of those sessions, and I learned to love jazz.

We ran a folk club in that same space for some years, and my first public performance took place there. By the early 60s there were more groups than fingers on both hands based in Reading. There were weekly R&B gigs, with visiting genuine blues legends at the Olympia Ballroom in London Street and the Shades coffee bar the home of Reading's folk scene; yet we all still dreamed of escape from what we then perceived as the claustrophobia of Reading.

We could all 'see how beautiful anything could be if only [we] could change it.' That was our dilemma. For my friends and me, the solution and solace was sought in music. You will find mention of many

* This passage is actually a quote from Raoul Vaneigem's *The Revolution of Everyday Life* (Rebel Press, 2006).

of them in this book; they and the music we made together and shared together saved our lives, and that of many others in Reading, and was eventually the key to our escape.

As I write this, I learn that another Reading musician and friend, Terry Clarke – singer, guitarist and songwriter, and one of Reading's great talents – has left the planet. Although not as widely recognised as some of the others, Terry Clarke was one of the great ones who shared our journey; a romantic and a 'bridge builder' – building bridges between imagination and reality. My preface is dedicated to his memory.

Sail on, sail on, sailor.

Mike Cooper
Valencia, Spain, April 2020

1. Introduction

In the summer of 2013, two newly retired teachers began work in Reading's only dedicated second-hand record shop, the legendary Sound Machine. Initially, Mike and Adrian were under the impression that this was the first time they had met. It turned out they had both played for the same football team back in 1972 and 1973 and, perhaps more relevantly, had attended many of the same rock concerts at the Town Hall, the Top Rank and the University. Cue lengthy reminiscences about the excellent French support act to Arthur Brown's Kingdom Come at the Town Hall in the spring of 1973, Ange, and whether Rory Gallagher's appearance in 1972 was recorded for his subsequent *Live In Europe* album (it wasn't).

They were not alone: men of a similar age (and they were usually men, but not exclusively) would pick up an album in the shop and exclaim loudly, 'Blimey! Haven't seen a copy of this for a few years. Saw them at the University back in 1970, and the lead singer fell off stage drunk. They were great!' Mike and Adrian began to think, why not write something about the experience of popular music in our town and relate it to the country as a whole? Say, between the years 1966 and 1976?

Two Sound Machine regulars and record collecting obsessives were also eager to contribute. Austin Matthews, a frequent contributor to a variety of music publications and arch-champion of the under-appreciated and obscure, undertook to oversee the massive edit the original project required and the new shape it demanded, finally adding his excellent sketches of the local musical heroes of the age.

Having attended far more rock festivals than would be considered safe and, mercifully, having emerged with his sanity intact, Rob Callaghan was the ideal person to research and write about our own Reading Festival. His excellent contributions can be read in Chapter 8.

So why choose this particular period? Mike and Adrian were both in their teens or early twenties at that time, young men eager to be associated in some way with the emerging rock culture. These years begin with the rise of psychedelia and end with the dawn of punk. Neat. In between, a plethora of new styles emerged: progressive rock, heavy metal, glam, reggae, funk and disco – and they were just the start.

Reading, like so many towns during this period, was being transformed, both socially and physically. Areas of the town were pedestrianised, ring-roads constructed, shopping centres erected and many a street bulldozed in the name of progress. Trolley buses disappeared and the M4 finally arrived, as did the InterCity 125. The town lost its traditional industries as Reading's three Bs – biscuits, beer and bulbs – disappeared, their places taken by the new tech industries as Reading became the hub of the UK's Silicon Valley. Not a bad trade-off, really. Meanwhile, Reading Football Club remained rooted to the old Third and Fourth Divisions, playing from their dilapidated Elm Park home, despite the brief but superlative performances of the genius Robin Friday.

In March 1968 the *Reading Chronicle* ran the headline 'Reading is Dragsville' when it reported a statement from the Caversham Park Village Association, and a 1963 article in the Reading University Students' Union newspaper, *Shell*, had asked its readers, 'Is Reading more than a place to shop or wait for the bus?'. It went on to suggest that 'To some of the older, more blasé students, their University town is about as exciting as its drab Victorian façade.' Mike and Adrian would beg to differ.

In 1974, however, the BBC confirmed for many Reading's status as Britain's average town by screening a ground-breaking documentary series, *The Family*, purporting to portray the life of a typical working-class family, the Wilkins. It was certainly an honest picture, but whether it was typical or not was hotly debated at the time, with many feeling that it was an insult to both the town and to the working class, orchestrated by a patronising, intellectual elite. True or not, Reading's 'Average Town' card had been well and truly stamped.

In 1966 the pop music package tour still reigned supreme; half a dozen chart acts playing twenty-minute sets around the country's concert halls and cinemas, but rarely in Reading. This town feasted on a diet of the best R&B bands of the era – Georgie Fame, Zoot Money, Geno Washington and their ilk – guaranteed to deliver a good time. And local bands, with sets comprising all the Motown, Stax and James Brown classics, packed out the church halls across the county.

But times they were a-changing. Bands that just played other people's material began to struggle, and many local bands found themselves being overlooked in favour of the new-fangled mobile discos who would play all the hits for a fraction of the cost or bother. Although soul and R&B acts continued to pack out venues like the Top Rank, at the University and the colleges a new music flourished. It generally discouraged dancing, so audiences tended to sit on the floor, the better to appreciate the supposed musical proficiency of the new sounds, but also (let's be honest) because the drugs had changed; amphetamines were out and cannabis, more likely to induce calm reflection perhaps, was in.

These eleven years witnessed the growth, and the zenith, of the town hall and university rock circuit. Artists as diverse as David Bowie and Black Sabbath, Pink Floyd and B.B. King would be appearing at a Students' Union in your town. But as the popularity of the music grew, fewer and fewer universities or civic amenities were geared up to cope. The PA systems and lighting rigs grew to a gigantic size, so much so that Reading University's New Union struggled to accommodate The Who and their massive technical presence by the end of 1971.

This book is an attempt to catalogue the popular musical landscape of a typical British town during the years from 1966 to 1976. Reading is more fortunate than some in that it has a university, a couple of colleges and an annual music festival, but less fortunate in not having a decent-sized concert venue, at least until the Hexagon opened in the late 70s.

'And how exactly are you going to make this book interesting for people like me?' asked Adrian's university-bound stepdaughter, Mia.

Her coruscating remark begged a response. Read on.

2. The pre-1966 music scene in Reading

In the early 60s Reading was on the up, exemplified by the completion in 1960 of three blocks of flats in Coley, each 15 storeys high – the tallest buildings in the town! There was a growing amount of entertainment for thrill-seeking youngsters in the shape of a pair of dance halls, a batch of cinemas and the Town Hall which offered a diverse range of theatre and music. There were also popular meeting places like the Café Olé and Honey Bear coffee bars.

And, it was on the up musically. Ok, so The Beatles never played here, unless you count the legendary appearance of John Lennon and Paul McCartney at the Fox and Hounds in Gosbrook Road, Caversham, on 23 April 1960. The pub was owned by Paul's cousin Bett and her husband Mike. Paul and John visited them in the Easter holiday, pulled pints and performed twice. They called themselves The Nerk Twins and made their own posters. There is now even a blue plaque commemorating the event.

In December of 1963, The Rolling Stones appeared at the Town Hall. There followed shows at the Olympia in January and March in the new year, the latter soon after the release of 'Not Fade Away', their first Top 10 record. Other rising stars followed, including The Yardbirds (St John's Ambulance Hall, November '63 and the Olympia, April '64), The Animals (Town Hall, January '64), The Who (Olympia, November '64, prior to the release of their first top tenner, 'I Can't Explain'), The Kinks (Majestic, June '64), John Mayall's Bluesbreakers (Olympia, September '64), The Moody Blues (Olympia, October '64) and Tom Jones & The Squires (Olympia, April '65), amongst many others. The stars were beginning to shine over Reading.

A musical revolution was taking place. American rock 'n' roll had taken the country by storm in the 50s, the UK contributing, with notable exceptions, callow imitators. An exception, but never a rock 'n' roll singer anyway, was Reading's own hit-making celebrity Alma Cogan ('The girl with a giggle in her voice'), a former student at St. Joseph's Convent School.

Now it was our turn. Out of traditional jazz was born skiffle, a home-grown craze likened by many to punk in its simplicity and a first step for many of the 60s stars to come. The new decade may have begun quietly enough, with the nation's own pop stars Frankie

Café Olé in London Road

Vaughan, Adam Faith, Cliff Richard, Petula Clark and those peerless instrumentalists, the hugely influential Shadows, holding their own against the American tide, but skiffle had done its job. Everyone wanted to be in a group.

Local beat combos began to emerge, such as The Trends, The Raiders, The Dominos, The Wild Ones, The Storms, The Moquettes and The Gangbusters, fronted by Cal Vincent, a baker's roundsman. Young people had time and freedom on their side, more money, and no conscription. The economy might at last be recovering from the war, but the shadow of The Bomb loomed dark on the horizon. Time to party with these guys in a church hall near you!

With R&B a favoured musical style, aficionados could visit the St John's Ambulance Hall in Chatham Street where such luminaries as

Audience arrive at the Shades coffee bar on Minster Street for the folk club night, early 60s

The Cyril Davies All Stars and Alexis Korner appeared in 1963. They greatly influenced local luminary Mike Cooper, who formed his own band, Blues Committee, in 1963. Another important local character, this time studying at the University, was a young vocalist, Arthur Brown, frequently found singing with local jazz bands, including that of Reading legend Dave Morgan. The town had a smattering of jazz venues, including a regular club, the Latin Quarter on Bridge Street, and a host of fans in the town and at the University.

The folk scene in Reading was also booming, with Mike Cooper instituting a club at the Shades coffee bar, and others being set up by enthusiasts across the town. This scene was instrumental in nurturing musicians who would later taste international success, including

Mike and Sally Oldfield and Marianne Faithfull, who made the leap to fully-fledged pop star with the Jagger/Richards-penned number 'As Tears Go By', a hit on both sides of the Atlantic in the summer of 1964.

Ballroom dancing continued to be widely enjoyed, with many 'Schools of Dancing' dotted around the town such as Courts, the Studio and the Alexandra. The major venues all continued to provide the opportunity for young people to show off their skills with 'Modern Dancing' nights once a week.

The Moquettes and Platform Six were probably the town's top bands from this pre-'66 music scene. Both were snapped up by record companies in the hope they would hit the big time; sadly neither did. The former released the improbably titled 'Right String Baby but the Wrong Yo-Yo' on Columbia Records in July 1964, but management problems apparently scuppered any hope of success. Platform Six released 'Money Will Not Mean a Thing' on Piccadilly Records in July 1965 but were not helped by the appearance of promotional fliers across town announcing, 'Get Your Kicks From Platform Six'. This apparently caused alarm with the management at Reading Station, who were concerned that drug dealing might be taking place there!

Diversity and innovation were flourishing in the dance halls, clubs and coffee bars of the town – as they were across the nation – and would continue unabated for a very considerable time.

3. The early years (1966 – 1968)

1966

A British teenager in 1966 may perhaps have been entitled to believe that they were positioned at the epicentre of the world, certainly as far as popular culture was concerned. Mini-skirts and mod styles dominated the high streets, The Beatles and The Rolling Stones the singles and album charts, and English football the world! But an awful lot of new ingredients were about to be added to the mix, and not all of them from these islands.

Articles about a new drug, LSD, and the mind-altering state that it induced started to appear in the press, and it was very quickly reflected in the music being produced. Meanwhile, the newspapers were full of the Vietnam war, the struggle in Rhodesia and the awful Aberfan disaster. Mao's Cultural Revolution was in full swing, as was the US and Soviet race to put a man on the moon. And rivalling The Beatles to the title of Most Famous Face on the Planet? Cassius Clay.

But for many young people, the greatest thing about the year, besides England winning the World Cup, was the Top 20. A single ear plug from a tiny transistor radio tuned to one of the pirate stations, reception variable at the best of times, gave VIP access to a golden age of British popular music as The Kinks, The Who, The Yardbirds, Small Faces, The Beatles and The Stones thrilled us with their ever changing, restless music.

Losing the Olympia Ballroom to the spreading craze for bingo at the end of 1965 had been a blow to the town's youth. However, for those who had religiously made their way to the top of London Street for a lively night out, most of the same bands could still be seen across town at the Majestic. With the R&B/blues phenomena still in full swing in 1966, such artists as Georgie Fame, The Graham Bond Organisation, Zoot Money's Big Roll Band, Chris Farlowe, The Steampacket with Long John Baldry, The Birds (with Ronnie Wood on guitar in his pre-Stones days) and Geno Washington and the Ram Jam Band all appeared regularly. One notable appearance was that of the Paul Butterfield Blues Band on 7 November 1966. From the Fillmore West, San Francisco, to the Majestic, Reading! An appearance by game-changers Cream at the Majestic in October 1966 was

Georgie Fame who filled The Majestic in the mid-60s

perhaps an indicator of the direction that popular music was taking, for better or worse. They managed to clear the dance floor.

A small multitude of jazz and folk clubs contributed to the musical diversity on offer in the town. The Upper Deck at the Ship, with an emphasis on trad jazz, hosted such luminaries as Stan Tracey, Chris Barber and Terry Lightfoot, and the various folk clubs saw performances from rising stars like Mike Cooper, Maddy Prior and ex-busker Don Partridge.

The Amboy Dukes photographed at the Abbey Ruins in Reading, 1967

Gerald T. Moore & the Memphis Gents with their tour van!
(Moore in jumper fourth from left)

The wonderfully named T-Pot Cosy, onstage in the mid-60s

More pop-oriented bands were still to be seen at the town's other venues, often promoted on the strength of a recently released record. In 1966 the Glow Room presented The Herd (whose singer Peter Frampton would, ten years later, release one of the biggest-selling albums in history, *Frampton Comes Alive!*) along with The Riot Squad and Alan Price. At the Excel Bowl you could catch The Bystanders (later to become Man), and at the Rainbow Hall you could watch The Falling Leaves and local recording stars, The Amboy Dukes.

Local bands were still frantically busy delivering good times to youth clubs, church halls and social clubs. Amongst the most popular were The Mackandas, who were fully booked every weekend, appearing in such places as Emmer Green Youth Club, the Roebuck on Oxford Road, Coronation Hall, Woodley, and the Gillette Social Club on Basingstoke Road. The Memphis Gents, The Dark Ages, T-Pot Cosy, The Delta Sound, and The Outcrowd were just five of the many other local outfits plying the same circuit, but a hint at what was around the corner could be seen in a June 1966 advert in the *Reading Chronicle* for a discotheque at the Glow Room. It would take

The Mackandas, which featured John Stannard, photographed in the mid-60s a year or two before local bands were competing with DJs and their piles of 45s.

Meanwhile, away from music we saw the end of Reading's fourth B: bricks (and tiles), the manufacture of which had been a longstanding industry significant in the town since mediaeval times, even giving Tilehurst its name. No longer would Reading folk see the aerial cable car that carried the buckets of clay from the pits off Norcot Hill to the brickworks in the area now known as the Potteries estate.

1967

The year opened with a bang in Reading as Pink Floyd heralded the dawn of the psychedelic age with an appearance at the University in January. Sadly, the Majestic, mainstay of the mods, closed as a music venue and, like its old rival the Olympia, re-emerged as a bingo hall. The Excel Bowl also shut its doors, this time for refurbishment. Three of the town's top venues had disappeared. Thankfully, in October the owners of the Majestic, the Top Rank Organisation, opened their new suite at Station Hill adjacent to the newly completed Western Tower. This would become the town centre's leading music venue for many years, with top soul artists and rock bands appearing.

The folk clubs ticked along gently but there also seemed to be an appetite for larger-scale events at the Town Hall, and several took place. Reading's own Mike Cooper and Bill Boazman featured, alongside such artists as Al Stewart, singer Anne Briggs, The Young Tradition, The Jug Trust, Gerry Lockran and many more besides.

The Reading University Rag record for this year featured student Janie Grote, who also appeared in one of these concerts. Janie told us, 'I was at Reading University reading Zoology and used to be a frequent singer at the University's folk club. A friend had a relative with a recording studio in Birmingham who offered to record the songs for free, and we promoted it through the folk club. The record is pretty awful, and the cover is even worse!' Oh well.

Local bands were finding work harder to come by, and even The Mackandas had called it a day by April. A few, like The Amboy Dukes and The Memphis Gents, remained popular, the former even performing at the Ashmead School Fete (where some of them had been pupils) while in contrast The Memphis Gents were offered an opportunity to tour the UK as backing band for the great American soul

Mystery band (Is this The Storms?)

singer Edwin Starr, which they were delighted to accept. There was, however, plenty of soul in the town, with performances in some of the smaller venues from The Soul Trinity, The Soul Invaders, The Soul Bucket and The Soul Reason! By year's end, newer bands started to emerge who embraced the new psychedelic trends. The Rite Amount and The Livin' End could now be found where The Little Angels and Sounds In The Night might once have played.

Elsewhere, Brian Epstein died and Joe Orton was murdered, as was Jack 'The Hat' McVitie. Homosexuality in the UK was no longer illegal, and abortion was legalised. Colour TV was introduced, the Arabs and Israelis fought the Six-Day War, the *Torrey Canyon* slopped crude oil over Cornwall, pirate radio was outlawed and replaced by Radio 1, the Ford Escort was introduced, Concorde unveiled, Muhammad Ali stripped of his titles, and we all watched *Magical Mystery Tour* on Boxing Day and then had to convince our sceptical parents that it was quite good and no, The Beatles hadn't gone completely mad.

1968

Top artists covering a range of popular music styles appeared in Reading venues this year. It was not a bad place to live either, apart from the dreadful traffic problem, soon to be addressed by, ahem, the opening of the IDR. The football club was going nowhere fast, but almost everything else one could wish for in a provincial British town was here, with plenty of the top retail outlets and an abundance of pubs. Sadly, the trolley buses had but a few months left to run. Reading was also learning to embrace its multi-cultural future with a growing West Indian and Asian population.

A wider picture revealed the seeds of discord being sown as Enoch Powell delivered his Rivers of Blood speech. The bloody war in Vietnam dragged on and got bloodier, and England pulled out of the Test series with South Africa over the Basil D'Oliveira affair. On a more positive note, the race to put a human on the moon entered the final furlong, and Stanley Kubrick released his epic 2001: *A Space Odyssey*, a film so far ahead of the field that it still manages to look futuristic 50 years later, and then there's that suitably psychedelic ending.

Musically, the town was booming. The University was by now firmly established on the rock circuit and was also attracting some of the biggest names in jazz. The new Top Rank had quickly become the place to see chart-bound pop and soul artists. A range of pop sounds could be heard at the Thing-A-Me-Jig Club, though a bit lower down the ladder of success. Jazz continued to have a strong following, with the University attracting world-renowned musicians. Folk music flourished in the town's clubs but also in concerts at the Town Hall and the University. The sounds of blue beat and ska filled the Cosmo Club, local bands the youth clubs and church halls.

The Top Rank had initially opened with discos and house bands such as The Ronnie Smith Band, who briefly included a certain Rick Wakeman.

Whilst traditional jazz, performed by the likes of Monty Sunshine and Ken Colyer, was the mainstay of the Lower Ship's Upper Deck, there was often some slight variation, like the two notable appearances by American blues singer and pianist Champion Jack Dupree, resident in the UK by this time. Since artists like Colyer frequently played the blues, this was no great departure stylistically. Over at the University the jazz club continued to thrive, with one particularly eye-catching gig featuring American sax player Coleman Hawkins.

The Town Hall was no longer staging rock concerts, but folk music events continued. One held in March included John Renbourn, Al Stewart, Bill Boazman and the Electric Laundry. Although the *Reading Chronicle* was not wholly impressed, their critic noted that John Renbourn 'stole the show with a demonstration of his superb guitar technique which has made him the country's leading Blues guitarist'.

Over at Reading Technical College, the student magazine *Ancora* reported that the Jazz and Folk club there 'has functioned well with performances given by Mike Cooper, Bill Boazman and Derek Holloway in the lunch hour,' although it seems the club was not that well supported by the students, for the article continues, 'It is a sad fact that few of them have chosen to take advantage of the opportunities which these (gigs) offer.'

Local boys The Amboy Dukes and The Memphis Gents continued to gig furiously far and wide although, according to The Dukes' Dave Kislingbury quoted in an *Evening Post* article, the band were 'furious that their record company Polydor had let them down by not producing sufficient quantities of their latest release "Judy In Disguise" to meet the demand.' Following their successful tour with Edwin Starr, The Memphis Gents returned to Reading and could be found playing in many of their old familiar haunts amongst them, the Thing-A-Me-Jig Club, Mary Magdalen Hall at Kentwood Roundabout and Coronation Hall, Woodley. Towards the end of the year they changed name to The National Hot House and continued playing in local venues.

There was also a new generation of ambitious local bands playing the smaller venues. Among them were Dry Ice, a six-piece band whose versatility helped sell them. As bass player Colin Solman said when interviewed for the *Evening Post*, 'Everyone in the group can play more than one instrument, and as part of our stage act, we stop, change our instruments and carry on playing.' Fair enough.

Others playing the local circuit included those wild rockers Cannery Row, blues band The St James Infirmary, The Studd, and Blue Flagg, whilst enduring outfit The Chordets, formed by sax player Doug Buller in 1962, was still hanging in there and would continue to do so for many years, with Doug always at the helm.

Reading University 1966–1968

Before launching into an overview of the ever-dynamic, ever-changing music scene at Reading's colleges and the University, a quick word is necessary about the Reading University Students' Union newspaper, *Shell*. It was published monthly during term time, finances permitting, and is an absolute mine of information. Often with a new student editor each term, content would have reflected issues deemed relevant to its readership, the student body. Between 1966 and 1976, it vacillates wildly in tone between a kind of junior version of *Tatler* (lots of pictures of students in dinner jackets and ball gowns), *Oz* magazine (lots of pictures of topless students and dope stories), *Socialist Worker* (lots of pictures of students with clenched fists, marching) and *New Musical Express* (lots of pictures of rock bands).

Still published today, but since 1986 called *Spark*, the paper provided (and continues to provide) a platform for Social Committee to advertise upcoming attractions, clubs and societies, and halls of residence. Published letters were often lively, as were the album and live music reviews, although until 1970 these were almost exclusively about jazz on campus. There are gaps, however: occasionally there would be no money to publish, so most of 1970, for example, has become something of a dark age to research. At other times the editor may have had little interest in anything musical, or Social Committee failed to get its act together to provide information – or perhaps they, too, had run out of money and the term's entertainment consisted of a handful of desultory discos.

One debate highlighted in the paper runs right through the period this book covers: should University concerts be open to non-students from town? As early as the spring of 1966, under the headline 'Youngsters Invade Hops', *Shell* reported that students might in future be asked to produce NUS cards to gain entry: 'A youth of about fourteen and his girlfriend of about twelve came to the bar and asked for two vodkas and lime... We must find a means of stopping these people from getting in.'

Not too hard, you'd have thought; but increasing numbers of thefts and some particularly unpleasant trouble later in the decade made the University consider the issues surrounding security even more seriously. By the time most musical events were being staged in the New Union on the Whiteknights campus, the trouble for Social

Committee was that many of the staged events were far from sold out and they were happy to admit outsiders. In fact, they even took the trouble to advertise events in the national music papers, and much debate raged in *Shell* about the amount of money lost on some individual bookings.

Neither Reading Technical College nor Bulmershe College had anything as comprehensive as *Shell* – their publications being printed on a more ad hoc basis – so information about the musical entertainment provided at the time comes either from personal experience or can be a bit sketchy. Shared events like Rag Week would be advertised in *Shell*, however. Reporting on the woeful organisation of some events over 1967's Rag Week, including a Julie Felix concert at Bulmershe, the paper did note one lone success: 'On a wet night, and with no publicity, the Tech dance had a full house of 400 and had to turn people away. The Tech needed no publicity because their dances are known all around town.'

On 14 January 1967, Pink Floyd made the first of their three appearances at Reading University, this first one in the oak-panelled magnificence of the Great Hall on the London Road site. Destined to produce the biggest and most successful stadium shows on Planet Earth and record sales to match, they were yet to record their debut single 'Arnold Layne'. The Floyd arrived as the standard-bearers of the burgeoning British psychedelic scene and the darlings of all that was hip in London club circles. While all this played out well enough in the trendy clubs of the capital, it didn't necessarily travel too well, provincial crowds being somewhat baffled by the rather introverted Syd Barrett, the band's hyper-trendy King's Road apparel and the whole psychedelia trip. Geno Washington and the Ram Jam Band this certainly was not.

Judging by the letters subsequently published in *Shell,* the Reading gig divided opinions in the same way punk would ten years on. 'Wild' Bill Hutchinson wrote:

'Boos from the back contrasted with applause from the front... Their performance seemed to consist of a complete annihilation of music... amplifiers were so loud that most of the notes were distorted... It was rather like having one's ears glued to a pair of maracas and then being put into one of those centrifuge machines they train astronauts in.'

He conceded that at least it was something different. Not so a trio of students from St Patrick's Hall:

'We would like to express our disgust at the appalling performance given by the Pink Floyd. How could people dance to such an offensive din? [They] were so cacophonous that the most cunningly random-noise-making machine could hardly have been more oppressive. We congratulate the element among the few remaining at the end who gave vent to their indignation by booing.'

In the following edition of *Shell*, Social Committee compère Chris Heyworth conducts a sturdy defence of the booking and, in so doing, demonstrates the importance of the University in helping to enable popular music to evolve from being merely a throw-away adjunct of consumer capitalism concocted in Tin Pan Alley to that of an art form in the hands of a progressive few, and as important as jazz had been to a previous generation:

'The fact that the Floyd have lately been receiving great attention [in the press] without having released a record, and have been playing to capacity audiences in London clubs, would be reason enough to book them, without the consideration that if Reading had not engaged a psychedelic group, Social Committee could be open to the criticism that their policy is un-progressive and, one is tempted to say, reactionary.'

The Fine Art department's decision to book The Sex Pistols some ten years later, playing to about 20 people, is perhaps covered by this same broad-minded philosophy. Well done Reading!

The problem was that, to the uninitiated, this Pink Floyd gig was just another dance, the 'Coming Up Hop', post-Christmas jollity. If, as a student, you were used to forking out to dance to the likes of Zoot Money's Big Roll Band and Geno Washington and the Ram Jam Band (which you might well have done by attending the Union Ball back in December 1966), then the Floyd were going to come as a bit of a shock. Zoot and Geno, Long John Baldry with Bluesology at the Childs Hall Formal in February of that year, and the University's very own home-grown heroes, The Soul Proprietors (who played everywhere across the campus in 1966), were all aiming to get you dancing the night away and giving you your money's worth. In November, the Great Hall played host to Lee Dorsey – more top class soul and

SOCIAL COMMITTEE
presents their
FUTURE ENTERTAINMENT

11th OCTOBER
ECLECTION
AND
QUICKSAND

25th OCTOBER
CLIFF BENNET
AND
CARAVAN

22nd NOVEMBER
MARSHA HUNT
AND WHITE TRASH
AND GRAPHITE

10th DECEMBER
FAMILY AND
FAIRPORT CONVENTION
(negotiating)
and several others to be arranged
There will be a discotheque every Friday, sometimes progressive and sometimes Boppy, but always danceable.

Social Committee hope that the Union Ball will be different this year—no tradition, crazy decorations and no D.J.s unless people REALLY WANT TO !

An advert in *Shell* from 1969 showcasing a diverse selection of gigs

another evening likely to have had everyone going home feeling their money had been well spent, perhaps especially so when reflecting on the gig years later: the supporting act was David Bowie and his band The Buzz.

As popular music developed over the last years of the decade it began to be taken more seriously, and not just by the music press. The Jimi Hendrix Experience and Cream were having strings of hit singles that channelled a mix of jazz and blues through the kaleidoscopic lens of psychedelia while revealing their virtuoso talents at tinnitus-inducing volume. Bob Dylan's bridge to a new songwriters' universe saw the next generation queuing up to pay the toll: Pete Townsend, Ray Davies, Paul Simon, Brian Wilson, and Mick and Keith were just the tip of a very creative iceberg.

Jazz had once occupied this ground; this was where serious lovers of modern music were to be found. Bearded, sandaled and bohemian, they marched to ban the bomb, attended the first outdoor festivals, and may have partaken of the occasional 'jazz' cigarette. Many of them were university students, and very many Reading University students were jazz fans. It is no wonder that, as well as hosting some of the biggest stars, the University helped further the careers of some of its own undergraduates. Chart topper Arthur Brown, the infamous 'God of Hellfire', had an inkling that a professional career as a singer might be on the cards when he sat in with Acker Bilk at a New Year's Eve dance and was informed by the chart-topping clarinettist that he might make the grade.

Undergraduate John Marshall, drummer for Soft Machine and a host of other jazz fusion bands through the 70s, gained a formidable reputation sitting in the drum chair for visiting stars to Jazz Club. The jazz correspondent for *Shell* had this to say about him:

'We have one superlative stylist in Jazz Club... His drumming is a joy to anyone following the current British jazz scene. My opinion is that [he] is one of the best jazz drummers I have heard in this country. And part of the credit for this must go to Jazz Club: for Jazz Club is not just somewhere to go on a Monday evening – it is THE place to go.'

Undergraduate pianist Pat Brandon had been instrumental in setting up, or at least reinstating, a jazz club as a permanent entity, either in residential halls' junior common rooms or in sympathetic pubs in the town, Ye Boar's Head in Friar Street being one such, the Upper Deck at the Lower Ship being another. The aim was to provide a platform for student jazz musicians looking for an audience and to invite professional guests. Visits in 1966 by Stan Tracey, the Don Rendell/Ian Carr Quintet and Chris McGregor's avant-garde warriors suggests a high standard was maintained, although a Mr Thomas, writing for *Shell*, warned of the Tracey visit, 'He is certainly the best jazz pianist in the land but will have to attract a large audience on Monday if the Club is to be financially able to continue.'

The middle years of the 1960s were good times for jazz on the Reading campus. An appearance by esteemed tenor saxophonist Tubby Hayes in St Patricks' Hall brought a large crowd and all parties seemed well satisfied with the evening, which, unfortunately, ended on rather a sour note: it seems that a rather well-soaked Hayes rightly took offence at his singer, Joy Marshall, being told to 'shut your trap' by the Domestic Bursar. Said Bursar and Hayes squared up to each other and had to be pulled apart; the police were called. Hayes and his entourage departed for London. *Shell* takes up the story:

'The Bursar, having just urged Hayes to leave, now reported him as being drunk in charge of a car. The police left in pursuit, apparently in the direction of Swansea and all points west. [All this] trouble [was] caused by the confrontation of two incompatible ways of life.'

Arguably the jazz highlight of the decade was the decision by the BBC to film one of their *Jazz goes to College* concerts for BBC2 in the Great Hall, featuring Max Roach+4, with Freddie Hubbard on trumpet, and tenor saxophonist Sonny Rollins. The packed house, which included just about every notable jazz player on the British scene come to pay homage to these greats of post-war music, seemed well pleased. Reviewer Simon Puxley for *Shell* commented that 'Their performance...was flawless. Reading is unlikely to be privileged with a jazz event of such quality again.'

The difficulty for many was that jazz now seemed to represent the old, established order of things. Your teachers liked jazz. The great Coleman Hawkins' appearance in the Great Hall to 'a very small audience' early in 1968 perhaps illustrates the decline in interest. Within a year a musician of the calibre of Miles Davis would be asking why it was that he was reduced to playing the same old circuit when these young, white upstarts' albums went platinum. Solution: lose the suit, change the sound, change the audience, don't compromise with the music, release the awesome *Bitches Brew*. Result: massive album sales, everlasting widespread fame.

Post-Pink Floyd, Social Committee clung to that sense of adventure that has served them so well in the eyes of posterity by trying to book The Jimi Hendrix Experience for the Vice Chancellor's Ball in the summer of 1967. However, Hendrix's management had quickly grasped the value of the contract they held. It may have been possible back in December '66 to pay five bob to see him play the Thames Hotel in Windsor – but not now. Terry Hanby, Organising Secretary of Social Committee, said about the failure to secure the booking, 'Hendrix's agents have been contacted but they would not give us a definite price. We were offered a bad contract, and it would be foolish to be trapped into paying up to £400 at this stage.'

Jimmy James & The Vagabonds were booked instead, along with Herbie Goins & The Nightimers; both first-rate soul/R&B outfits, but unlikely to prompt letters of indignant incomprehension to *Shell*. Fellow soul stalwart Zoot Money, a 'face' on the London club scene who had mixed with both Hendrix and Pink Floyd, saw the writing on the wall and ditched his Big Roll Band for the full-on psychedelia of Dantalion's Chariot. This short-lived experiment produced one classic single and a performance in the Great Hall in November, a couple of weeks after a reportedly stupendous appearance by The Jeff Beck Group.

The University might have been slow off the mark with Jimi, but they secured The Who three times over the next three years. The first of these, an appearance at the Union Ball at the tail end of '68, was in conjunction with rising stars of jazz rock Colosseum, along with poet (and co-writer of much of Cream's material) Pete Brown & His Battered Ornaments (or Scattered Ornaments, as *Shell* would advertise them). Absolutely at their peak, The Who's appearances at the University would book-end the releases of arguably the three greatest albums of their career: *Tommy*, *Live at Leeds* and *Who's Next*, the latter their finest hour.

Childs Hall pulled off something of a coup in October of 1968 in presenting Jethro Tull at their Informal. The same week saw the Hall promote Scottish hell-raiser Alex Harvey, his name soon to be preceded with 'The Sensational' – with good reason. Childs was having a good week.

Social Committee presentations, Rags, Formals, Informals, Bonfire Hops, Freshers' Hops, Balls for a multitude of occasions: they all played relatively safe with their booking policies post-Floyd, and securing Hendrix to play the Vice Chancellor's Ball was, frankly, always a bit optimistic. After all, the objective was to have fun and dance, and break even at the very least. Booking chart toppers Amen Corner in February of 1968 was therefore an expensive risk, partly offset by offering tickets for sale in the town. *Shell* reports that 'Tickets were sold out completely by 8.30 and many disappointed students had to be turned away; profiteers cashed in by selling tickets at black market prices.'

A sense of outrage was often expressed by contributors to the paper when things went wrong with the organisation of events, which seemed to happen quite a lot. And why wouldn't it? These were willing amateurs with little or no experience facing up to the machinations of the commercial music business and the wiles of Joe Public. The kids done good.

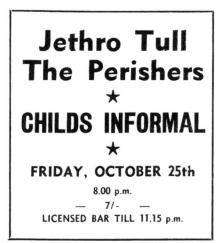

Somewhat of a coup for Childs Hall at Reading University in securing this early booking for Jethro Tull in 1968

The venues of Reading

Reading wasn't such a bad place to live for a music-loving teenager, so where might you have gone to indulge your passion?

Reading Town Hall

The Town Hall was not used for pop or rock events on a regular basis until the early 1970s – with some notable exceptions. The most eye catching of these was an appearance of The Rolling Stones on 27 December 1963. They were supported by local band Kay & the Koronets and Dave La Kaz and the G Men from Bournemouth, who boasted a young Al Stewart in their ranks. The show was staged by local novice promoter John Boman. He told us,

'I was only 18 at the time, so could not sign any contracts, the legal age being 21. I persuaded John Manning my local newsagent to sign them instead. The Stones turned up in their van, having battled through a pea-souper of a fog, and although I had planned to bring them in through a corridor under the stage, I was so excited

Reading Town Hall shook to the sound of heavy rock bands in the 70s

when the van pulled up, I brought them straight in through the main doors. The cost was a mere £200 for two thirty-minute sets.'

Steve Eagles, guitarist with Kay & the Koronets, remembers: 'The place was absolutely packed. I took a photo of Mick [Jagger] in the dressing room we shared with them.'

The Town Hall really took off as a rock venue in the early 70s, playing host to as many as a dozen shows a year and becoming a featured destination for bands touring the UK such as Roxy Music, Leo Sayer, Rory Gallagher and King Crimson. The audience was seated, at least theoretically, which set the Town Hall apart from the town's other venues.

The Olympia

London Street was a busy thoroughfare into town and boasted a lively social scene. However, the building of the Inner Distribution Road (IDR) in 1969 rather cut it off. Its numerous restaurants, pubs, coffee houses, shops and clubs gave it an atmosphere far removed from the traffic-choked backwater it has since become. Who could forget Tuttys the clothing store, where school uniform could be purchased on credit?

Number 75 London Street housed one of the oldest dance halls in town, the Olympia Ballroom. Originally a private residence, it became a ballroom during World War I and a favourite destination for all the big names in big band jazz right into the 50s. The 60s saw it switch allegiance to the sounds emanating from Liverpool: Billy J. Kramer, The Undertakers and The Merseybeats all played, enabling local acts like The Dark Ages, The Out Crowd and The Moquettes to appear as support. Paul Whiteway was a member of local crew The Jokers and proudly recalls opening for The Hollies and John Lee Hooker at the Olympia in 1965, while Mike Shonfield was a roadie with local boys The T-Pot Cosy, who supported The Searchers there:

'There we were, backstage, with these superstars who were top of the hit parade that week. I remember I spent most of my time trying to stop crazy, screaming girls from bunking in backstage.'

It was to the Olympia that The Rolling Stones returned on 5 January 1964.

During the mid-60s a concave ceiling was added to the ballroom, lined along its entire length with different-coloured neon strips. Alongside the new pop reality, the Olympia continued to function as a venue that hosted ballroom dancing and jazz.

By 1964 it had become a regular port of call for British R&B exponents like Georgie Fame & The Blue Flames, The Groundhogs, The Paramounts and many others. The involvement of London promoter and manager Rik Gunnell ensured a great turnover of bands at this time. On Fridays it became a different club, Leo's Cavern, with the likes of The Birds, The High Numbers (pre-Who), and The Moments (featuring a young Steve Marriott) playing. Reading's mods considered the Olympia their spiritual home.

At the end of 1965, bingo won out and it became the new Olympia Star Bingo and Social Club. When that lost its sparkle, the building was first converted to a cinema, then to a private banqueting facility; eventually, in 1999, it became a live music venue again, The Matrix. Sadly, on a March night in 2002, with urban garage outfit Heartless Crew on stage, it became the scene of a double shooting. The club closed immediately but re-opened just two weeks later. In September it lost its licence but seems to have further re-opened after an appeal by the owners.

The Majestic

The Olympia's major rival during the early 60s was the Majestic Ballroom on the Caversham Road. 'The Maj', as it was affectionally known, was built in 1936 as the Reading Corn Exchange, where merchants from around the country would have arrived with sacks of corn and laid out samples on tarpaulins covering the floor before bargaining would begin.

Unusually, the Majestic doubled as a roller-skating rink during the daytime before transforming into a ballroom at night. Around 1960 it was taken over by the Top Rank Organisation who gave it the Majestic name, and it soon became a leading music venue hosting top names on Monday nights as bands could be booked more cheaply then than at weekends. It also hosted ballroom dancing nights, with the legendary George Watkins Orchestra in residence.

In 1966, with the Olympia finished as a music venue, promoter Rik Gunnell transferred his Reading operation to the Majestic, showcasing the likes of Geno Washington and the Ram Jam Band, Zoot Money's Big Roll Band and Jimmy James & The Vagabonds on a weekly basis. It rapidly became the hip place for home-grown R&B. In January 1966 an appearance by Georgie Fame broke the attendance record, the doors being closed well before the start of the show. Top names like Long John Baldry and Steampacket (who included Rod Stewart), Cream, The Who and The Kinks all played there. Music promoter Martin Cole has this memory of Cream's appearance:

'The first gig I went to was Cream at the Majestic, who played two sets, and a Tamla Motown disco. There were possibly a thousand people in there but when Cream went on most left and there were about 40 of us crowded around the stage. I remember Ginger was as high as a kite!'

By 1967, Top Rank were looking to relocate to their new, purpose-built development on Station Hill and – as had been the fate of its old rival, the Olympia – the Majestic was revamped as a bingo hall. It became a music venue again in the mid-80s, playing host to the likes of The Stone Roses, before becoming Washington Heights in 1990 and later RG1. It closed in 2002 and was demolished three years later.

The Top Rank Suite

The grand opening of the new Top Rank Suite took place on 27 October 1967 with a charity ball that included top comedian Dave Allen. The building consisted of a lower floor with licensed bars, a buffet bar and dance floor with revolving stage, and an upper balcony overlooking the stage on three sides. The *Reading Mercury* of 23 July that year reported that 'The size of the suite, as well as lighting, heating and ventilation, can be altered by the push of a button.'

It wasn't long before top soul acts from the States were seen on the Rank's stage as they worked their way around the organisation's circuit – Jimmy Ruffin, The Detroit Emeralds, The Chi-Lites and many others performed there, as did top pop bands The Sweet, Mungo Jerry and, in 1972, The Beach Boys. Big rock names also featured, including Free, Family and Uriah Heep.

For the biggest dance hall in town it was economically viable to book the bigger names although, as this was the early 70s, it was a dance hall in which everyone sat cross-legged. The University even hired the Rank on several occasions for their Rag Ball as neither the Great Hall nor the New Union building at Whiteknights Park could hold the numbers to make booking the likes of Humble Pie or The Kinks a profitable proposition. By 1983 the Rank was closed as a music venue; it too was converted to a bingo hall. The newly opened Council-run Hexagon theatre and concert hall went some way to compensate for the loss, but the Top Rank was sorely missed.

112 London Street

The Alexandra Ballroom at number 112 London Street, almost opposite the Olympia, was a smaller venue. Originally a dance studio and residence of the Alexandra School of Dancing, it sported mirrored walls that had to be covered on music nights. By 1966 it had become increasingly popular as a music venue, with UK band The Birds (featuring future Rolling Stone Ronnie Wood) appearing weekly. Members of the band could often be found hanging out in the Honey Bear, a nearby coffee shop, before and sometimes after their shows.

Known then as 'The Alex', this London Street venue changed its name as regularly as it changed promoters. In 1966 it was the Glow Room, with top-notch bands continuing to play there, including The Riot Squad and a whole mess of local heroes. In the early months of 1967 it became the Rub-A-Dub Club but suffered no loss of quality: Chris Farlowe, among others, performed there. Later in the year came a further change: it became the New Wheels Club with Eric Clapton and Cream playing there on their return to Reading on 25 June 1967; somehow they managed to squeeze their massive amplification onto the club's tiny stage.

By 1968 the venue had become Crawdaddys, with appearances from the likes of The Moody Blues and The Orange Bicycle. By now it was also hosting reggae and soul artists under the Cosmo Club banner.

In September 1970, 112 London Street saw a further change, to the Windrush Club. Numerous bands, legendary in rock circles, whose scarce but highly collectable records are now absurdly expensive, appeared here during the venue's very short lifetime. Step forward High Tide, Mighty Baby, May Blitz, Writing On The Wall, Principal Edward's Magic Theatre and Bram Stoker. The promoter was the legendary Ron Watts, 'Godfather of Punk', as he was later known, and lead singer with perennial support act Brewer's Droop. It was advertised as 'Reading's New Progressive Rock Club' but, sadly, its Thursday evening sessions only lasted until January.

In 1973 it re-opened as the Caribbean Club, offering somewhere for the town's West Indian Community to meet, drink, play dominoes and listen to music. It was run more along the lines of a social club rather than a nightspot, but economic necessity soon led to it being hired out for events.

By the late 70s, as the Paradise Club, it once again became a regular music venue, which has continued in that vein as the After Dark since the early 80s.

The Thing-A-Me-Jig Club

In January 1967 the *Reading Chronicle* announced a new club opening in Minster Street, the Thing-A-Me-Jig Club. Set up by two entrepreneurial students at Reading University, the aim was to foster closer social ties between the University and the town. The article quoted one Roger Chree as saying, 'The aim of the club is to provide premises for the 18–30 age group to meet in a lively and sophisticated atmosphere. This is just what Reading needs. Somewhere for the in-between group'.

Some rivalry may have existed with the equally recently opened Rub-A-Dub Club, as large adverts in the local press appeared simultaneously for both. However, a few months later Rag Day 'difficulties' and police intervention forced the Rub-A-Dub Club's closure, having played host to The Shevells, Chris Farlowe and The Mojos during its short life.

The Thing-A-Me-Jig Club spanned two floors in a former morgue, with the entrance in Earley Place, off Minster Street. It proved to be a successful venture, operating initially as a disco but soon stretching to accommodate live acts such as The Downliners Sect, with artists like The Strawbs appearing on folk nights.

Both the décor (orange and purple) and the *Reading Chronicle*'s report on the opening night were very 1967: 'It is graced with a small army of pretty girls working in the bar and reception area.' The club was the brainchild of students Charles Trevor-Roper and Peter Briggs; the latter hoped 'that club membership (30 shillings p.a.) will be from a cross-section of the community – business people, nurses and students.'

By October, the University's Students' Union magazine, *Shell*, reported under the heading 'Clean Club for Town and Gown' that the Thing-A-Me-Jig Club was

'Not a here-today, gone-tomorrow affair. It is not a centre for drug pushing, and, because of its organisation, could never be so. The club is willing to entertain any person who is reasonably dressed. It will not stand for tee-shirts and jeans. Not only is it ideal for couples, it is also a place where girls can go, maybe in groups, and really enjoy themselves.'

This refreshing attitude, radical for 1967, reflected the club's origins within the University. Reverting to a disco, the club ran until 1976, when it became Harvey Wallbangers, and finally – rather appropriately – Bones, during the punk era.

The Excel Bowl/River Room

In the early to mid-60s, ten-pin bowling was big business in the UK, with the Excel Bowl, at the junction of Caversham Road and Vastern Road, leading the way in Reading. Above the lanes was a dance floor, and a local agent, Jim Cookson, was approached to book the acts. London promoter John Edward was also later involved.

One band seen here regularly during 1967 was The Bystanders from South Wales. They would soon be far better known to rock fans as Man, becoming stalwarts on the club and college circuit and recording a slew of albums for United Artists. Another popular outfit to appear regularly was Pinky and The Fellas, who were often billed as returning 'by popular demand'. I guess we'll have to take their word for that. During its lifetime the venue was renamed The River Room.

Smaller colleges, ballrooms and halls

With the growth of the 'college' circuit during the late 60s and early 70s, the University, Bulmershe College and Reading Tech offered many top rock bands to satisfy the insatiable musical thirsts of the towns' long-hairs. Access to these gigs was never guaranteed, however, unless you were the holder of a precious Students' Union Card.

In the early to mid-60s there were two smaller ballrooms in the town centre that hosted live music. They were the Oxford Ballroom and the Rainbow Hall. The former could be found at the end of Eaton Place. Built in the 1930s, it was used mainly for modern and ballroom dancing and was apparently quite small, often crowded and very, very hot. The early 60s saw dances featuring local bands like The Wild Ones and The Raiders, but as far as we know it does not seem to have hosted any major names before closing at the end of 1965.

£ s d

at

BRIDGES BALL

on

FRIDAY, JUNE 21st

The Nite People

The 1958 Rock 'n Roll Show

featuring Freddie " Fingers " Lee
The Caribbean Coloured Steel Band and
The Cambridge Footlights

BARS   NIGHT CLUB

TICKETS from BRIDGES 154 and 75

An advertisement for a summer ball at Bridges Hall, Reading University from 1968

The Rainbow Hall was unusual in that it was on the second floor of what was then the Co-op building in West Street. Groups did play there occasionally though. Tyburn Ashes was one of them, playing in May of 1966; the band included one Ray Dorey, who would later find fame with chart toppers Edison Lighthouse. On the same evening, another largely unknown outfit, The Shindigs, also appeared, featuring Ian Paice, later of proto-metal leviathan Deep Purple, on drums. By November 1968 the Rainbow had become a restaurant and cocktail bar.

There are some surprises too. St John's Ambulance Hall in Chatham Street played host to The Roosters with (a young) Eric Clapton, The Yardbirds and Graham Bond (with future Cream co-founders Jack Bruce and Ginger Baker), all during 1965.

Youth Clubs

For the under-18s it was off to the local youth club for a dance. In these pre-disco days, live bands provided the music, mixing the hits of the day with the staple dance fare of R&B and Tamla Motown. Dave Plummer played guitar with one of the hardest-working of these groups, The Mackandas, and his diary for 1966 included appearances at venues throughout town, Emmer Green and Woodley, and taking in the Gillette Social Club, the Technical College and the Majestic as well. Local girl Janet Davis told us, 'I put on dances for the church youth club in St Luke's Hall on Erleigh Road. I know we had The Amboy Dukes and The Trends. Of course, we only served soft drinks!'

Whilst a number of dances such as these did appear in the 'What's On' pages of the local press, the vast majority didn't, their existence being publicised on youth club noticeboards, pinned to telegraph poles, stuck on lamp posts or simply passed by word of mouth. Coronation Hall, Hemdean Road Youth Club, St Matthews Youth Club and English Martyrs Youth Club often advertised their dances in the press however, especially if they were promoting a band from out of town. Welsh boys The Iveys were one such outfit, travelling from Wales to play St Matthews Youth Club several times, possibly because their fan club secretary Sylvia Collins lived just across the road. An excellent young band learning their trade, they went on to be signed to The Beatles' own label Apple, later becoming Badfinger.

The Lower Ship (aka The Horse and Barge), location of the Upper Deck

Levee Camp Moan at The Crown

The Target

1971 saw the opening of the Target pub, under the Butts Centre, with steep steps leading you down into an abyss. It proved a hugely popular destination for rock fans and provided a regular venue that enabled local and more national bands to get a feel of the business. Very crowded, very loud and very smoky, the Target proved to be a massively popular venue to catch live music five times a week. It had one serious drawback though: the entrance steps were by the side of the stage which meant that if you arrived after the band had started, every head in the room watched you descend from the heavens. Girls in short skirts needed nerves of steel. Different times...

Other Reading pubs

The town centre was awash with pubs during the 60s and 70s. Folk clubs could be found tucked away in a few of these. Amongst those who found space for them were the Elephant in Market Place, the Cross Keys on the corner of Gun Street and St Mary's Butts, Ye Boar's Head in Friar Street, the White Horse in Caversham Road and the Red Cow in Southampton Street, whilst the Upper Deck at the Ship in Duke Street was the Reading home of trad jazz.

Others dipped their toes in if the landlord was a fan. The Crown in Crown Street was where Martin Cole honed his management skills, organising a blues club. Regulars were Bracknell's own Levee Camp Moan, whose sole album has since become highly collectable. Martin went on to promote The Clash's first US tour. It is indeed a long way to the top if you want to rock 'n' roll.

Many other pubs tried their hand at the live music lark, but by the late 60s mobile discos were taking over the scene. Let's face it: they were cheaper and a lot less trouble. The gigs started to dry up for groups that played mostly covers. Rare venues like the Target nurtured young bands with original material and kept the flag flying until the advent of pub rock and punk blew open the pub doors once again. And everyone wanted a piece of that action.

The middle years (1969–1972)

1969

Even as the town faced up to the destruction required to make space for the IDR, the bands played on. Many of us attempted to grow our hair to the lengths our rock idols were achieving, but were faced with seriously stiff opposition from teachers and bosses. Others were headed in the opposite direction: skinheads. These were often ex-mods, their new identity intentionally setting them apart from the supposed scruffiness of the longhairs. Ben Sherman and Brutus shirts, Dr Martens and Levi's Sta-Prest trousers with braces were all part of the look, accessorised with brogues and Crombie coats for nights out. Favouring the sounds of rock-steady, blue-beat and ska, theirs was a determinedly working-class statement, and whilst we all usually got on perfectly well as individuals, some skinheads despised the air-headed intellectualism of mostly middle-class, woolly-minded, dope-smoking layabouts. Sad to say, as a card-carrying member of the latter, you avoided them like the plague on nights out!

The University was now a fixture on most rock bands' touring schedule, while its folk and jazz clubs continued to be well supported. Bulmershe College was busy too, with Status Quo on the bill in June promoting their latest release, 'Are You Growing Tired of My Love'. The Town Hall also added its name to this schedule with The Move appearing in March, just as the delightful 'Blackberry Way' went Top 10. They used to smash up TV sets on stage in their early days – performance art and all that – but let their excellence as a band make its own statement about their worth. In support were Reading favourites The Iveys, rising from the town's smaller venues as they progressed towards becoming major stars.

The Town Hall proved a popular setting for folk music, including an appearance by jazz-folk luminaries Pentangle with Reading folk club regular, guitarist John Renbourn. Another evening featured Roy Harper, Jackson C. Frank and Heron, with ex-Memphis Gent Gerald T. Moore. Guitarist and founder member of Heron, Roy Apps, was Entertainments Secretary at Reading Technical College. Unsurprisingly, Heron appeared numerous times.

Ben E. King and The Freddie Mack Extravaganza brought the authentic sounds of soul back to the Top Rank, and the University

tudor Lodge folk duo

enquiries to:
J. STANNARD, 57, PITTS Lane, EARLEY, READING. 62546.

A promotional flyer for Tudor Lodge when the band was a duo featuring Lyndon Green (left) and John Stannard (right) from 1969

booked the venue for an Informal, presenting a band who would go on to define British blues-rock: Free. Early days – these eighteen-year-olds were promoting their first album, *Tons of Sobs*, though the *Reading Chronicle* was a bit sniffy about the turn-out: 'Good music – poor support.'

The White Horse Folk Club presented Reading's own Tudor Lodge, at this time a duo comprising John Stannard and Lyndon Green. Other pubs had a go, such as Ye Boar's Head, where Reading singer Eric Blackburn teamed up with Bulmershe College student John

Grace to become The Boatmen. In an *Evening Post* interview John suggested,

> 'What we want is to develop our own style. We do try to adapt to our audience, but a pub audience is about the hardest you can have. They haven't paid to hear you and if you're no good it's your own fault and there's nothing you can do but go away and improve.'

Other pubs where they could be seen regularly were the Fox & Hounds, the Three Tuns, the Jolly Anglers, and the Ferryman in Whitchurch, so they gave it a good go. Out at Aldermaston the fine Kennet Folk Club at the Stag's Head was now advertising regularly in the Reading press, with jokey singer Derek Brimstone amongst the performers. Over at the Crown, local promoter Martin Cole had started his own blues club.

Meanwhile, back in Caversham, the Excel Bowl's dancehall re-opened as the River Room, but rather than dancing to ambitious un-knowns, patrons were entertained by artists who, while well known, had enjoyed their moments of glory some time back. The list is quite impressive for all that: it includes Billy Fury, Millie, Clinton Ford,

The Jolly Anglers occasionally hosted folk acts

Billie Davis, and The Settlers. Obviously they were hoping to attract a somewhat older crowd.

No doubt the Town Hall was packed for a February appearance of The Amboy Dukes, supported by two other local favourites, the pop/ rock of Oedipus Complex and the lighter touch of The Shoreline Set, regulars across town. Oedipus Complex, a three-piece act, released two singles in their short existence, with the second, 'Up, Down, Run Around' in the shops in May. Lead singer Felix Terry had this to say to the *Evening Post* in April: 'We have got the long hair bit coming in now and we have changed our style of music too. Call it a sort of progressive pop. It's west coast music really.' What, like the Grateful Dead then?

By the end of the year the first part of the IDR opened from Castle Street to Caversham Road; but of much, *much* more importance was the fact that Hickies provided a free list of the singles released each week!

1970

Musically, 1970 was the year in which the seeds sown in the 60s began to bear fruit. Deep Purple's *In Rock* and Black Sabbath's eponymous first album built on the foundations laid by Led Zeppelin to create heavy metal, and progressive rock really began to flourish. The Moody Blues topped the album charts with *A Question of Balance*, Pink Floyd had their biggest-selling album to date with *Atom Heart Mother*, Yes broke through with their third album, as did Emerson, Lake and Palmer with their debut, and Miles Davis released the double album *Bitches Brew*.

The Mexico World Cup confirmed Pele as the greatest player of all time, and the third Isle of Wight Festival was the biggest event of its kind. Having topped a stellar bill, Jimi Hendrix was dead within a month, followed a short time later by Janis Joplin. The movie *M.A.S.H.* used the Korean war of the 1950s to explore the morality of Vietnam. Back home, it was Mick Jagger's time to shine, starring in both *Performance* and *Ned Kelly*.

Deep Purple headlined at the University in January, six months before releasing aforementioned album that would define them, and the Top Rank had Free again, just as 'Alright Now' hit the top of the charts. Mungo Jerry and, surprisingly for this smart venue,

The Strawbs visited the town's venues a number of times

the anarchic Pink Fairies also appeared, but it was for their stand-out soul presentations that the Rank really stood out, with Jimmy Ruffin, Nicky Thomas and Jimmy James & The Vagabonds all on show this year.

You thought the Reading Festival began in 1971, right? Well, there was an unofficial one held on the Richfield Avenue site the previous year. Stewart Harding told us that the 'unofficial' 1970 festival was a small affair cobbled together by a bunch of hippies: a smattering of local bands with names lost to the mists of time, and a suggestion that Hawkwind also played. About a hundred folk turned up, along with a few bikers from the nearby Viking Café. It kicked off Saturday evening, resuming on Sunday with a visit from Harold Pendleton, or-ganiser of the National Jazz and Blues Festival who was seeking out a new location. Seems like he found one!

'The Spring Thing', an outdoor event that seems to have been better organised was scheduled at Reading Football Club's Elm Park home for April. With a line-up featuring Fleetwood Mac, Chicken Shack, Colosseum, Vivian Stanshall, Christine Perfect and Mike Cooper, it looked like a winner. Our own Mike Warth was in attendance; having bought tickets, he and his mates sat on the terracing opposite the stage set up on the centre-circle and awaited kick-off.

'Unfortunately it was raining so it was announced that the start needed to be delayed. Oh well, we thought, but it continued to rain heavily and with the stage open to the elements it was decided the event had to be cancelled and we all trudged home totally deflated, with the rain still falling.'

Two folk concerts at Caversham Court were luckier with the weather: one was an evening of music in aid of Oxfam, the other an all-day affair billed as 'A Five Hour Folk Concert' featuring Don Partridge, Jake Thackeray, Mike Cooper, Heron, Eric Blackburn and former associates of Mike Oldfield, Mellody Tickell.

The Town Hall gave us The Strawbs this year, but little else. Bulmershe took a chance with Scottish rockers Writing On The Wall, as did the Tech with fellow Scots Marmalade. The Thing-A-Me-Jig Club ramped things up big-time, however, presenting The Crystals, The Drifters, Jimmy James & The Vagabonds, Rufus Thomas, Herbie Goins & The Nightimers and The Ronettes over the course of the year. They balanced this with some decent pop/rock from Matthews' Southern Comfort, Harmony Grass, Steam and Katch 22 – the latter six times!

The River Room turned away from presenting old pop artists, having teamed up with a London management outfit, the John Edward Agency, to promote new bands from outside the locality. They included the Sir Percy Quintet, Portrait, Spencer Mac, Crazy Paving and the very popular Heatwave. The weekly dances held at the club provided an alternative destination to the Top Rank.

In September, 112 London Street witnessed the birth of a new club, the Windrush, named to honour the West Indian origins of the venue's owners and overseen by the estimable Ron Watts. As noted earlier, it was a short-lived affair that played host not just to the cream of the underground, but also to American blues legend Muddy Waters (see Chapter 4).

The Cosmo Club continued to present occasional visiting reggae artists such as The Fabulous Mohawks, while just down the hill from 112, Alice's Restaurant, rather surprisingly, advertised live music on Fridays. Meanwhile, the River Buoy Club at the end of Caversham Bridge, probably best known in later years as a casino, also offered live artists, among them The Strange and The Frost. Reading Rugby Club gave us The Shoreline Set, The Chordets and Tudor Quorum, whilst the Ryeish Green Club offered Pale Explosion and The Kroude. What were all these bands like? Any guesses, anyone?

The Red Cow in Southampton Street re-started its folk activities in August and gave us the great Shirley Collins and Tony Rose, as well as resident performers The Shambles and hosts Pete and Alison Nalder.

1971

In a year during which the news was dominated by the deteriorating situation in Northern Ireland, the music scene in the UK continued to demonstrate the extraordinary talents of the citizens of these islands to innovate and experiment with forms that often had their roots elsewhere. Exponents of hard rock, heavy metal and prog released some of their finest albums, and long-established acts such as The Rolling Stones and The Who produced arguably their greatest works: *Sticky Fingers* and *Who's Next*. But the year also saw the glam rock phenomenon begin to take over the charts in the contrasting guises of T Rex and Slade, and David Bowie released what many believe to be his best record, *Hunky Dory*. We'll gloss over Middle of the Road's 'Chirpy Chirpy Cheep Cheep'!

Mid-way through February, decimal currency was introduced and caused problems for older people. Evel Knievel was a big star, and Smokin' Joe Frazier defeated Muhammad Ali. The Russians established the first space station, Salyut 1 – sadly, the only three crew to enter it successfully were all killed on their return journey to Earth. The Open University was also launched – on TV.

In Reading, 1971 proved to be a most significant year for music as it gave us the first 'official' Reading Festival in June. Three days of fun, frolics, booze and narcotics – oh, and not forgetting loads of great rock bands (see Chapter 8). Actually, the year was a good one for a variety of outdoor concerts, with King's Meadow, Caversham Court, the Forbury and the Abbey Ruins all offering music in the fresh air.

The first outdoor events of the year covered an intriguing few weeks in the spring when the bunch that organised the Richfield Avenue gathering of 1970 made use of the Abbey Ruins on Saturday afternoons to allow anybody who wanted to come along to sing, play, listen or dance. Very much in tune with the hippy way of thinking, these impromptu happenings attracted a certain type of young person – hippies! A generator was acquired and Hickies, the music shop, provided microphones and amplifiers. Referred to as the 'generator shows', these events are fondly remembered by those who were there.

The same group were given permission to use Forbury Gardens on 13 June and organised a free concert by the distinctive rock band Quintessence. A large crowd attended on a beautiful summer's day, with much clambering onto the Maiwand Lion statue and general chilling out.

Just over a week later, the band Heron played the Forbury, but this time not from the bandstand. Mike Warth recalls:

'A Sunday morning's revision for A Level Geography was proving particularly tedious so I jumped on my bike and cycled at great speed to the Forbury in time to catch Heron in full swing. A fair-sized crowd were happily lazing on the grass soaking up both the sunshine and the sounds. Wonderful.'

Elric at one of what became known as the 'Generator Shows' held in the Abbey Ruins in 1970

In early July, what was expected to be one of the South of England's largest folk music gatherings was staged at King's Meadow. Some familiar names, both national and local, were booked. Among the former were Dave and Toni Arthur, Jonathan Kelly, Tony Rose, Heron and, from America, Tommy Makem, while regulars from the local clubs included Mellody Tickell, Rod Garfield, Pete Nalder and Johnny Collins. The *Reading Chronicle* reported,

'A success musically, particularly as local artists had played such a prominent part, but the poor attendance had been a great disappointment.'

In September, Caversham Court was the scene for the next outdoor happening, when a collection of folk and blues artists performed alongside the 'Father of British Blues', Alexis Korner.

Indoors, the University continued to impress with a seemingly endless number of top names from across the UK, America and the world. The other Higher Education establishments, Bulmershe and Reading Tech, also chipped in with some fine sounds, including Status Quo at the former and, at the latter, Audience, a fascinating outfit who had played the University at the tail end of the previous year and were to be a highlight of this year's inaugural Reading Festival. The folk club at the Tech continued with their Tuesday lunchtime sessions, as reported in the college's magazine *Mushroom*. In March, the magazine noted that an Arts Evening arranged by the students was 'highly successful and included a performance by Pete Nalder, a lecturer at the College, who was assisted by his friend Peter Wass on guitar, cello, concertino, bandurria and a Meccano motor and paraffin can.' The magazine informs us that 'The principal guests were Heron who with their usual skill extracted the maximum possible performances from guitars, percussion and organ.'

Over at the Top Rank, soul and pop fans were entertained by top acts like Jimmy James & The Vagabonds, Arthur Conley, The Tams and Jimmy Ruffin, with reggae artists including The Pioneers and the very poppy chart regulars Pickettywitch.

The Town Hall opened the year on what some might regard as 'safe territory', with concerts by jazz trumpeter Maynard Ferguson, The Spinners, classical guitarist John Williams and the popular Ralph McTell. Towards the end of the year there was a noticeable change in direction as some seriously heavy rock bands were scheduled. These

Good Habit photographed at Highgate Cemetery in the early 70s. Mike Warth has fond memories of the band playing in Reading.

included the mighty King Crimson, Uriah Heep, Stray, Americans McKendree Spring on a UK tour, and The Groundhogs (twice). Adrian Moulton was there: 'The 'Hogs dressed like their audience; long, lank hair, denims and T shirts. They offered no "show" apart from the music, no banter and no stage effects, just an electric hurricane of pain and anguish.'

In fact, things were improving all over town. In March, the Thing-A-Me-Jig Club presented an Irish band playing only their second gig in England, none other than Thin Lizzy, fresh from an appearance at Ronnie Scott's the night before. The somewhat challenging Gnidrolog, Killing Floor, Good Habit and Scottish band Forever More were among the other higher-profile bands who appeared on the Thing-A-Me-Jig stage this year.

The Target pub's doors were flung wide in December on the edge of the newly constructed Butts Centre. Opposite, Tesco had been the first shop to do so in the Centre, opened by TV and radio DJ David

Jacobs amid much publicity and hullabaloo. The Target's opening was attended by Reading MP Dr Gerard Vaughan and Courage chairman Oliver Steele. It was to prove a massively popular town centre venue both for music fans and for the huge number of artists looking to make their mark (see Chapter 4).

As one new venue surfaced (so to speak), another disappeared: sadly, the Windrush Club ground to a halt in January, with final appearances by progressive rock bands Renaissance and Delivery. It's possible that the Cosmo Club either changed name or a new club simply took over the slot, as advertisements appeared for the Montego Ballroom, with reggae artists such as Jamaican Laurel Aitken on the bill.

A local outfit called Trellis topped the bill at the optimistically announced 'Dance of the Decade' at St Laurence's Hall. Others included an outfit by the name of Volume Two, who were Derek Miles, Colin Selman, Les Bond and Rick Gilbert, who later appeared at various dances in their new guise as Dateline. Newbury band Final Decision played for Reading Rugby Club and made a particularly memorable appearance – at least for them – at the Top Rank with DJ Emperor Roscoe. Demo recordings were made but went no further; the story of a thousand hopefuls.

1972

This was the year of Bowie and Roxy Music, and glam in general, and their influence was certainly felt among the flashier of us. T Rex and Slade took it in turns to top both the singles and album charts and prog continued its rise, with bands like Jethro Tull, Genesis, Wishbone Ash and Yes producing arguably their best albums, allowing those of us not totally besotted by Ziggy Stardust or Brian Eno to carry on wearing what we felt comfortable in.

The news was, as always, often grim. Idi Amin featured nightly as he expelled all Asians holding British passports from Uganda, the miners went on strike, the Watergate Scandal began to unravel and the situation in Northern Ireland (in the year of Bloody Sunday) was unremittingly awful, as was the news of the eleven Israeli athletes murdered at the Munich Olympics. Still, Bobby Fischer beat Boris Spassky at chess, Apollo 17 deposited the last astronauts to date on the surface of the moon, and *The Joy of Sex* was published. And

roxy

Roxy Music recently played at the town hall. After Keith Christmas finished telling his amusing anecdotes about how he 'turned on' some good traffic policemen (hey, wow!) and playing his extremely versatile guitar solo, preceded by some Pachable (citrus sweet 1950's style orchestral crap), swaying to the sinister sounds, as they then were, of Eno's moog (but it wasn't a moog, it was a synthesizer!), Roxy music appeared. After playing most of the stuff on their L.P. (called Roxy Music), they finished. The audience enjoyed it, anyway. Light work was synchronised with riff changes and 'the boys' occasionally broke into 1950's style manoeuvres with their instruments. 'Your man Manzanera's pretty good' said Herby, and indeed, Bryan Ferry's erotic Elvis Presley pornographic type gyrations didn't go unnoticed, nor did Eno's purple hair. 'Good Grief! We weren't expecting that!?!', said Bryan Ferry at their encore's beginning; they hadn't played Virginia Plain (their hit!). 'We don't know anymore numbers actually ... can you suggest any? ...what's that? ... could you say it a bit louder please? ...What's the name (VIRGINIA PLAIN)', Yer skinheads went mad (and I hope you're not rabied). Afterwards the local press photographer was overheard trying to get some 'pics' of the lads in the dressing room - 'actually they've got their jackets off now', said the manager - 'well look man, there's this fundamental difference between life and art' (fuck off). Shell got sent publicity photographs (ho ho).

S.T.P.

ROXY'S ANDY MACKAY (ex Reading)

Shell's early coverage of Roxy Music was surprisingly negative given Andy Mackay's connection to the University.

of course, Vietnam was still with us and provided the year's most shocking image: Nick Ut's photograph of a naked young girl running screaming towards the camera, burnt by napalm dropped from a South Vietnamese warplane.

By way of escape, 1972 was to prove, musically at least, a very exciting year in the town. The University led the way with appearances by The Doors, Steppenwolf, Hot Tuna and the Steve Miller Band. Rock fan Geoff Lawrence told us he had a difficult choice to make one evening: David Bowie at Slough College, Wishbone Ash at Slough Community Centre or The Doors at the University. He chose the latter and wasn't disappointed.

The Top Rank also hit the jackpot with appearances of two of the most influential of American bands, The Beach Boys in May and The Velvet Underground in December. The Beach Boys arrived promoting their *Carl and The Passions* album, but without Brian Wilson. He had produced the record but was in no fit state to tour. His brothers Dennis and Carl did though, along with Mike Love and Al Jardine, all stalwarts of the band. Unsurprisingly, the Rank was packed and the band excellent, by all accounts. The Velvet Underground, however, arrived in their last throes: having called it a day earlier in the year only to be resuscitated due to the success of a retrospective live album, *Live at Max's Kansas City*, a tour had been arranged hastily, and it included this December appearance. Masquerading session players filled the gaps, alongside the long-suffering Doug Yule, and as soon as the tour was over, that was it.

A list of visiting soul artists to the Top Rank included Curtis Mayfield, Wilson Pickett, Edwin Starr, The Detroit Emeralds, The Drifters, Mary Wells and Donnie Elbert – all big, big stars. Jimmy Cliff arrived hot on the heels of his film *The Harder They Come* (whose soundtrack is credited with kickstarting the reggae revolution), while ageing skinheads will recall The Pioneers and their reggae hit 'Long Shot Kick De Bucket'. Slade appeared with just the one number one song to their credit, but with plenty more to come; their spelling wasn't improving though, with their previous hit 'Coz I Luv You' swiftly followed by their latest release, 'Look What You Dun'. Glam rivals The Sweet would surely have belted out their recent hit 'Poppa Joe', but the really big hits were still a year away. Rock was also to be found at the Top Rank in the form of East of Eden and Family, who were promoting their most recent album releases, *A New Leaf* and *Bandstand*, respectively. Curved Air were due to play a double-header with East of Eden but refused to take the stage as the promoter couldn't pay them their full fee. 'Oh, how we booed them,' says Adrian, who was there!

The year saw an extraordinary number of the country's major artists blasting the mortar out of the brickwork at the Town Hall. Uriah Heep returned, with their best album *Demons and Wizards* just about to be released. And how satisfying it must have been for Andy Mackay to come back to the town just as his band Roxy Music were climbing the charts with their first release, 'Virginia Plain'. Irish guitar hero Rory Gallagher played a set that is now familiar to thousands,

Katch 22 were a Surrey band, though were frequently found playing in Reading in the late 60s

thanks to the *Live in Europe* LP, recorded on tour the previous month. Adrian was there that night and comments:

'The Bruce Springsteen of blues-rock guitar delivered lightning-speed stage thank-yous and song introductions as if he just couldn't bear to stop playing, even when the sweat was dripping off his old battered Strat. One of the best.'

Blues bands Savoy Brown and Chicken Shack (a double bill for 25p!) filled a grateful Town Hall, both outfits having successfully overhauled both their line-ups and their sound.

Bulmershe College offered us the progressive rock of Rare Bird, Patto and Supertramp and the US soft rockers Cottonwood, whilst Reading Tech went with Gypsy, around the time of their self-titled first LP. Both colleges would be reconsidering their booking policies within the year.

It was all change at the Thing-A-Me-Jig Club as they reverted to booking lesser known and, presumably, less expensive artists: Katch 22 were still regulars, but then we had Hampton Court, Putney Bridge,

Tobias Wragg and Smiling Hard. Who are these guys? The River Room began the year in similar fashion with Mr Kite and Happy Ending, but no other artists were advertised.

The Rugby Club still booked local talent like Final Decision and Black Ice, and live music enticed the diners at the recently-opened Monaco Restaurant in the Butts Centre, and at Dunes Night Spot. At the former, local act Swinging Affair, advertised as 'Reading's Number One band' (apparently), entertained the clientele. Dunes was a restaurant-cum-nightclub and booked acts like The Flirtations, still earning a decent living a good few years after their smash hit 'Nothing but a Heartache'.

Mike Cooper and his band The Machine Gun Co., a collection of some of the best Reading-based musicians and named after an album by German avant-garde saxophonist Peter Brotzmann, appeared at Caversham Court and the Progress Theatre, among others, with their unique mix of partially improvised jazz and country blues. The Cross Keys took over from the White Horse as the town centre's folk club, whilst out at Aldermaston, the Kennet Folk Club continued to present some interesting characters, amongst them Harvey Andrews, Noel Murphy, Callinan Flynn and the excellent Hunter Muskett.

Whilst we are out at Aldermaston, mention should be made of the annual CND march from Trafalgar Square to the gates of AWRE over Easter. About 700 people walked 52 miles over two days, and a rock festival was arranged to greet the marchers on their arrival. The *Evening Post* reported,

'Ban the bomb marchers arrived silently bearing 26 coffins and clutching handfuls of flowers. The black coffins – one for each year since bombs were dropped on Hiroshima and Nagasaki – were laid on the grass outside the gates and marchers filed past to stick daffodils in a six-foot-high CND symbol. Afterwards the crowd dispersed into a field opposite for a free pop concert.'

Mike Warth reports on that day,

'It was a breezy but dry day and the concert started a good while before the marchers arrived. I met a gaggle of friends there and we settled on the grass as Steve Peregrine Took, formerly an integral part of Tyrannosaurus Rex with Marc Bolan, was playing.

Progress Theatre

Mike Cooper & Machine Gun Company
and Terry Clarke in Concert
24th Nov · 25th Nov 8pm Tickets 50p
Ring Reading 84794

PROGRESS THEATRE THE MOUNT CHRISTCHURCH RD READING

TICKETS OBTAINABLE FROM GOLDERS BOOKSHOP KING ST

An advertisement for Mike Cooper's Machine Gun Company from November 1972

Graham Bond was next up, the band featuring poet and Cream lyricist Pete Brown. It was a powerful sound, with Bond's Hammond organ very much to the fore. Armada followed, their pleasing jazz-tinged prog album having to wait another forty-five years for a release. Hawkwind wound things up as only they could. My friend Ian Tyler recalls their music "floating off in the breeze".'

Nice, as Bob Harris used to say.

Reading University 1969–1972

In the Spring of 1969, Reading University demonstrated that it was very much a part of the zeitgeist, with the return of Pink Floyd and former chart-busting rhythm and blues exponents The Pretty Things, both booked for the Rag Ball. The previous year The Pretty Things had released the album *S.F. Sorrow*, subsequently hailed as the first rock 'opera', pre-dating The Who's *Tommy* by nearly a year. With support from The Gods, later to morph into the seemingly immortal beast known as Uriah Heep and booked after a stellar performance at Bulmershe College the previous year, one suspects that this might have been a ball stuffed with musical excellence, but precious little

Graphite formed at Reading University and every self-respecting local gig in the early 70s featured them as support!

dancing. And the same could probably be said about The Moody Blues headlining the Vice Chancellor's Ball in the summer, who had left their wild rocking days behind them and were already a long way down prog's parallel highway of sweet melodic pretension.

On hand to lend capable support to visiting stars over the next few years were Reading student heroes Graphite. Hardly a gig is advertised without their – by all accounts – excellent input. They may have failed in the end to crack the big time, but their gathered recordings, released some 50 years later, reveal a band steeped in the eclecticism of early progressive rock.

Although the new progressive rock was in its ascendency, jazz still flourished at the university, as did folk music, performed in ever-changing venues across the campuses of the University, Bulmershe College and Reading Tech. The traditional mix of floor singers and guests was the staple, but the bigger acts – those with a crossover appeal to a more general audience – needed more room. There were opportunities for this both within the new Students' Union in Whiteknights and the Town Hall. Fairport Convention appeared at the Student's Union towards the end of 1969, still high on the recent

---

SOCIAL COMMITTEE PRESENT:-
FAIRPORT CONVENTION
SKIN ALLEY
BARNABAS
in the New Union
on 31st January — from 8.30 till late
Tickets 10′- NUS and 12′6

An eclectic line-up at the New Union featuring Fairport Convention, 1970

success of the ground-breaking *Liege and Lief* album, and twice more over the years; the more esoteric but determinedly acoustic Eclection played the same venue in October. Pentangle, featuring ace acoustic guitarists John Renbourn and Bert Jansch were at the Town Hall as part of the annual Festival of Reading, with which the Reading seats of learning were heavily involved. Folk itself was changing and experimenting under the influence of progressive rock. Discounts were offered to Reading students who wanted tickets to see The Strawbs (a band in the throes of embracing full-blown prog with the imminent recruitment of the ambitious Rick Wakeman) at the Town Hall in January 1970.

Although he had been a regular at folk clubs across the town, by 1969 Al Stewart was a rather different beast. His album *Love Chronicles* had become a student favourite, with the singer's polite, very English delivery and erudite references setting him apart. He appeared on the Festival of Reading bill in June 1969, along with Maidenhead's finest, Heron, later to record albums on the Dawn label along-side Reading guitar-hero Mike Cooper.

Canterbury threw up enough new bands in the new progressive era to be considered a 'scene' on its own; two appeared at Reading University as 1970 dawned. Soft Machine, who first came to the University back in 1967 as slightly manic psychedelic improvisers, were in the process of becoming a full-on jazz outfit, the only thing standing in the way being drummer Robert Wyatt's vocal style, which conveyed a kind of middle-class English vulnerability. They were booked for the Bonfire Hop in 1970, but there was some concern that the trouble that had been experienced at a previous gig – involving the local Hell's Angels – might re-occur, and numbers were down (although perhaps the impossibility of dancing to the music of Soft Machine may have been the bigger deterrent).

Former Soft Machine man Kevin Ayers and his Whole World, featuring the very young guitar whizz Mike Oldfield, supported big league American band Bread in October 1970. *Shell*'s on-the-spot reviewer was not impressed by Bread: 'Unfortunately they spoiled it all by opening their deodorised mouths and singing. The noise took us back to the heyday of The Monkees, days which we would rather forget.'

There was only one singer on the circuit who sounded posher than Ayers, and that was Vivian Stanshall of The Bonzo Dog Doo-Dah Band. Perhaps best known today for its introductory announcements on Mike Oldfield's *Tubular Bells*, this anarchic collection of former art students headlined the Rag Ball in March 1970, and a rather truncated version of the band played the New Union – only a quarter-full – the following May.

Caravan, from the same Canterbury stable as Soft Machine but with added Home Counties stoner whimsy, never quite made the big league but played the University thrice at this time; the second of these occasions was in November 1970 during a break from recording their album *In the Land of Grey and Pink*, which is now regarded as a landmark of prog.

1971 proved to be an adventurous musical year for both the Entertainments and Rags Committees, kicking off with an appearance by American blues guitarist Johnny Winter. Folk legends The Incredible String Band came, as did ex-Cream drummer Ginger Baker and his Air Force, supported by Noir. Osibisa playing Wessex Hall back in the autumn and set to play the Union Ball in December shows another facet of the multiple musical trends current at that time. The prog-soaked audiences were generally a tolerant bunch, expecting to be both challenged and amazed by what was on offer. Ginger Baker's Air Force, Noir, Osibisa and a handful of others were multi-ethnic outfits playing jazz-rock powered by West African rhythms. You could dance to it, obviously, and as a result they usually went down a storm.

Both Emerson, Lake and Palmer and Yes, the two bands most people think of when prog is mentioned, were booked to play in the Union, though both fell through when their management were offered lucrative deals stateside. Still – getting T Rex to headline the Rag Ball was some coup; their single 'Hot Love' had recently topped the charts, and 'Get It On' was just around the corner. Mungo Jerry topped the bill for the Summer Ball, jazz-rock fusion bands Nucleus and Colosseum played the Union at opposite ends of the year, and Rory Gallagher the Union Ball. Graphite, meanwhile, continued to support on numerous occasions.

Undoubtedly the much-anticipated highlight of 1971 was The Who, secured for a New Union appearance in the Autumn. It was a struggle for the Union to accommodate the mountain of equipment these mega-stars were using, but they managed. By all accounts it wasn't the greatest of performances; *Shell*'s anonymous reporter wrote:

> 'We clapped in unison and shouted for more, but there was no more. [They] were apparently backstage for the next couple of hours discussing what went wrong. I've always been rather cynical of reports stating that The Who are the greatest… after this performance I am convinced that they are not.'

Ask any music fan with even the most rudimentary grasp of the history of popular culture who was the most influential rock band of the late 1960s, and there's a fair chance that The Doors will be cited. Their phenomenal popularity today is serviced by countless tribute bands touring the globe and the constant repackaging of their myth for the next generation. On Saturday, 13 May 1972, The Doors played Reading University. It is difficult to understand now, 50 years after the event, how this was ever going to work. How on earth were the band – irrespective of their unique instrumental sound – going to fill the void left by Jim Morrison, one of the most charismatic lead singers in the history of rock?

Well, by all accounts they managed to confound the cynics. At least a thousand souls were crammed into the New Union, initially sitting, until this became impossible. Playing as a five-piece, with added bass and rhythm guitar, they blasted their way through a set that mixed old favourites like 'Love Me Two Times' with material from their new album *Other Voices*. They were received ecstatically. Rich Allen, reviewing for *Shell*, commented, 'It would have been worth bankrupting Social Committee for the next generation or so to have had them play on all through the night and the next week. As it was, the buzz is still with me.'

When the band returned to the stage to play the inevitable 'Light My Fire', the audience roared their appreciation, forcing the band to deliver a second encore. A triumph of a gig, as it would seem – but how? Rich Allen, who had seen the band at both the Roundhouse and the Isle of Wight Festival, suggested that 'The Doors, far from being dead, have come alive in another sphere. Instead of living on past memories they have got together and progressed, applying their talents to a type of music they enjoy and play best.' It seems the place was overflowing with goodwill for the band to succeed – which it only did for a brief time thereafter. They *sounded* like The Doors, and maybe the people who came to pay tribute to their unique sound were just beginning to realise what they had lost. Without a doubt this was an event that the University was unlikely to equal for the rest of the year.

The old warhorse Ten Years After, stars of the movie *Woodstock*, played the Union in January '72, likewise the spiritually raga-soaked Quintessence, who played the following month. Both bands seemed as if their time had passed, and indeed it soon did. January also saw the rising stars of prog, Argent, at Childs Formal, their single 'Hold Your Head Up' soon to chart and – unbelievably – Van Der Graaf Generator, possibly the most intense of prog acts, headlining the Rag Queen Dance. Al Stewart headlined a Rags Folk event at the Town Hall and Humble Pie, with Steve Marriot on vocals, demolished a Rags gig at the Top Rank Suite. Lindisfarne were due to play but were replaced by our old friends Caravan. Over to *Shell* for an anonymous review: 'Caravan were an excellent substitute and immediately cleared away whatever cobwebs of skinheadery that might still have been hanging around.' Rags Committee had taken to booking the Top Rank for the odd gig. It held more people, which allowed the promoters to book more expensive acts. Normally associated with the promotion of the big beasts of soul, more readily accepted by working class youths looking for a good night out than the esoteric meanderings associated with so much of rock, this revealing comment suggests there was still some way to go to reconcile students with elements of the working class and their differing tastes.

A string of up-and-coming bands played in the New Union bar, including String Driven Thing and Amon Din (ex-Hawkwind). Lindisfarne finally made it to the New Union, as did the much-hyped Vinegar Joe with their twin vocalists Elkie Brookes and Robert Palmer. Finally, The Electric Light Orchestra, with just the one hit under their belt at this point, succeeded, according to *Shell*, 'in awakening a lethargic Reading audience to one of the best receptions a band has had at Reading; and that includes Vinegar Joe.' Onwards to '73!

The folk and jazz scene

Reading's folk scene

The American folk revival of the 1950s inspired interest in Britain's own musical heritage, resulting in numerous folk clubs being established across the country. London may have been at the centre of this new development, but Reading was not left behind.

This 'folk revival' was inspired by the likes of American musicologist Alan Baxter, folk song enthusiast A.L. Lloyd and singer Ewan McColl. In the UK the skiffle craze of the latter part of this decade introduced a new generation to American folk and blues. Perhaps particularly inspiring to a younger generation were the anti-establishment views of such American artists as Woody Guthrie, Pete Seeger, Bob Dylan and Joan Baez, though those performing in a traditional style also flourished.

By the 1960s there were at least a couple of clubs in and around the town centre where resident singers would perform. As J.P. Bean wrote in his book *Singing From The Floor: A history of British folk clubs*, the clubs often sprang up in, 'smoky rooms above pubs, bare rooms with battered stools and beer-stained tables, where the stage was no more than a scrap of carpet and a sound system was unknown.' Dark and dingy they may have been, but they provided a platform for the young artists who subsequently led the British folk scene revolution to hone their skills. Influential figures like blues guitarist Wizz Jones, singer songwriters and guitarists John Renbourn and Bert Jansch, the traditional folk singer Shirley Collins and guitar and fiddle player Nic Jones all played in the town's clubs during the latter part of the 60s and early 70s.

Run by enthusiasts, these clubs only needed to take sufficient money to be able to pay their visiting artists; their clientele were often young, politically-minded, duffel-coated 'beatniks'. It helped that Reading was on the route of the Ban-the-Bomb marches to Aldermaston that gained much publicity during the late 50s and early 60s.

Having been established in the earlier part of the decade, by 1966 the centre for Reading's folk scene was Shades coffee bar in Minster Street. The resident singer was Mike Cooper, a fine exponent of folk/

The White Horse, home of the Reading folk scene c.1966–1970

blues guitar and with many subsequent albums to his name. His first record, an EP, made with fellow Shades regular Derek Hall, was actually entitled *Out of the Shades* and released the same year. The promoter of the venue was Sid Lackington, who was instrumental in expanding Reading's folk scene. Another performer who appeared at Shades was Marianne Faithfull, who describes it as a 'Beatnik dive' in her autobiography, *Faithfull*.

In January 1967 the *Reading Chronicle* ran an article on Reading's folk scene.

'At the beginning of the year [1966] folk music could be heard at two established clubs, the Crown (in Crown Street) and Shades coffee bar. Mike Cooper and Derek Hall were resident in both, but by May both had closed. Mike Cooper then opened his own club at the Elephant Hotel in the Market Place which quickly became the centre of folk and blues in the town.'

In July 1966, however, the club moved to the White Horse in Caversham Road. Local musician Richard Cox-Smith recalls, 'It was in the old stable at the back – typical folk club; dark, dingy, freezing cold in winter but nicely cool in summer. The audience varied between about twenty and sixty, depending on who was playing.'

Another club was established in 1967, held in a candlelit room at the Red Lion in Southampton Street. It was organised by members of the Young Oxfam Group and named the Fennario Folk Club, who met on Wednesdays. Among the resident singers was the more well-known Bill Boazman (aka Sonny Black), and guests included Mike Cooper and singer Roy Bailey.

The University also had its own folk club, Ethnics, which had been in existence since 1963. By 1966 it was meeting in the Kennet Arms every Thursday with audiences of 60-plus. Posters dotted around the campus advertised guests. Presumably it was open to all-comers and not just students, but by the late 60s the club had moved onto the campus. The University also hosted a Folk-Dance Society that met regularly and who, in 1966, had the honour of beating the record in a folk-dance marathon, notching up 37 hours and 3 minutes of non-stop dancing in the car park of the Odeon cinema in Cheapside. Does this record still hold, we wonder?

Folk clubs came and went and, as an article in the *Reading Chronicle* in August 1967 indicated, the White Horse Club run by Sid Lackington was, with the University, the only survivor: 'Shrewd management has kept the club flourishing and top names continue appearing on a wafer-thin budget.' Among the guest artists were John Renbourn, singer-songwriter Johnny Silvo, Wizz Jones, Al Stewart, ace banjo player Pete Stanley and Nic Jones with his group The Halliard. One local trio who enjoyed a residency for a while consisted of Andy Holland, Chris Braclik and a certain Mike Oldfield, whilst another, Tudor Lodge, formed by local musician John Stannard, played at the club regularly. Their whimsical self-titled 1971 album on the Vertigo label has subsequently become a much sought-after collector's item.

Other venues held occasional folk nights, the Thing-A-Me-Jig Club for one, who in 1968 attempted a regular promotion on Wednesdays, starting with The Strawbs.

Folk festivals in the Town Hall, King's Meadow and Caversham Court helped to broaden the appeal of the music in the town. June 1966 saw performers including Davy Graham, Bert Jansch and The Strawberry Hill Boys (later to become The Strawbs) appear at the Town Hall in a concert organised by the University Folk Club, while another, organised by Fennario in February 1967, featured Mike

Cooper, trad folk singer Anne Briggs, and Bill Boazman, among others.

Folk festivals continued into 1971, most notably the one in July on King's Meadow, where singer-songwriter Jonathan Kelly, vocal group Therapy and local hero Gerald T. Moore's Heron were among those performing. And in the warm glow of September, Alexis Korner's appearance at Caversham Court was with Reading regulars Gerry Lockran, Cliff Aungier and Bill Boazman.

By 1971 the White Horse Club had relocated yet again, this time to the Cross Keys on the corner of Minster Street and Bridge Street. Singer/guitarist Richard Cox-Smith (who would soon be playing in the club himself) told us that going to the White Horse and the Red Cow was

'the highlight of the week for me as a teenager because it was cheap to get into; about 2/6d (12.5p). The nights always ran the same, opening with a bunch of "floor singers", a visiting guest followed by an interval, with the second half following much the same pattern. The guests were usually pretty good as in those days you could get the best down from London, especially with the White Horse being so close to the station.'

When asked how easy it was to book performers, Chris Smythe, who booked many for the Reading clubs, told us bluntly, 'You phoned them up and they would bite your hand off!'

Clubs came and went quickly during this era, and there was something of the do-it-yourself punk ethos about it: find a willing landlord with a spare room, contact the movers and shakers on the local scene, invite a 'name' and stick up the flyers. Local singer Eric Blackburn, who appeared regularly around the town, formed his own club in 1972, the Brick 'n' Fret at the Three Tuns on the Wokingham Road, with occasional guest singers that included Joe Stead and Tony Brummel-Smith.

By 1973 folk clubs were again springing up across the town, but they were often short-lived affairs. For example, the Bull in Broad Street presented 'Folk Rendezvous' once a week. At the Fox & Hounds, with its Lennon and McCartney connection, Bombadils Folk Club was created. Eric Blackburn's club at the Three Tuns thrived, while he also performed in others around the town, often at the Tudor Tavern in Friar Street. The Wynford Arms saw an appearance by the

The Red Cow (above) and a flyer for their folk night (below)

The Shambles which featured Patrick Wass and Brian Jefferson
as listed in the Folk Directory, 1973

much-lauded Carolanne Pegg during the venue's brief folk life. Ye
Boar's Head (lovingly known by locals as 'The Whore's Bed'!) also
dabbled briefly, with advertisements appearing in the local press for
a while.

Perhaps the fad for folk music was not that attractive to mainstream pub-goers after all; in any case the true believers were left
alone to enjoy their nights at the Cross Keys – shortly to move to the
Wellington Arms in Whitley Street – and the clubs at the University,
Bulmershe College and the Three Tuns, all of which offered high-
quality local performers and high-calibre guests who would go on
to become hugely successful on the scene over the next 20 years.
Patrick Wass played in a duo with Brian Jefferson during this period.
Calling themselves The Shambles, they had spells as resident
performers in the Red Cow and the Cross Keys. He neatly sums up
the scene:

'Folk clubs were great places to play. People would pay to listen. They paid attention and were appreciative. It's not like playing in a bar, it was like playing a concert.'

The Wellington Arms club, known as the John Barleycorn Folk Club, closed its doors in 1976, but re-opened two years later in the Cap & Gown, opposite the Reading Technical College. Local folk band Spredthick, formed by Hilary James and Simon Mayor also helped maintain the town's strong links with the genre throughout the 70s and beyond. Folk music lived on in Reading.

Reading's Jazz Scene

Prior to 1966, the Bull Inn on the corner of Broad Street and Cross Street was a regular venue but later, Jazz in Reading centred on the Upper Deck at the Ship in Duke Street on Sunday evenings. Here the emphasis was on trad jazz; such luminaries as the arch-traditionalist Ken Colyer, Chris Barber, Kenny Ball, Acker Bilk and Terry Lightfoot appeared on many, many occasions.

Local enthusiast Don Heaton told us, 'When I arrived in Reading in 1965, I first found jazz at the Bull in Broad Street with Jane Gwyn's Hot Six.' According to Don, not only was the jazz hot, but so was the food (!), an unusual feature in pubs at that time. He then moved on to the Upper Deck, where he saw numerous top names, including Chris Barber, George Chisholm and Humphrey Lyttleton.

Another local musician, drummer Eddie Page, told us that in the early 60s, jazz clubs could also be found at the Olympia and the Central Club, the latter situated in Percy Place – long since redeveloped – near Marks and Spencer. This Central Club may have also been called the Silver Bells Club at some stage, although we were unable to verify either name from contemporary records. Mike Cooper comments,

'There was a jazz club in Broad Street called the Silver Bells – a New Orleans Dixieland jazz gig was the first live show I went to. Then the Olympia Ballroom also had jazz groups visiting. I saw Ted Heath's big band there when I was 18 or so. There was also the Latin Quarter in Bridge Street, which was a really big venue run by some guys from London. They had jazz bands on the

Sunday afternoons which was really great. I listened to a lot of jazz there – many of the musicians were from Reading University and I also ran a folk club there for a while, very early on.'

Reading had its own trad jazz legend: trombonist Dave Morgan, whose band could be heard at almost every venue in the town throughout the 60s and 70s. As a 16-year-old he had been inspired by Chris Barber at the Town Hall. During the early 60s, a philosophy student from Reading University by the name of Arthur Brown linked up with the band to provide vocals for a short time. Dave Morgan's band enjoyed residencies at many a pub, including the Grenadier (which once stood in Basingstoke Road), and the Target, a venue normally associated with rock bands but with jazz featured on Mondays (including, in October 1973, the outrageous jazz-singing of the multi-talented Old Etonian George Melly). The band released an album in the 70s entitled *Jazz Merchants* and continued performing for many years. Around the same time, local musician Dave Price appeared at numerous venues with his trio, quintet or combo.

Another local traditional jazz band, formed in 1975, was The Sheffield Bottom Stompers. This moniker was taken from the hamlet of that name just outside Theale where they rehearsed and performed. They too released an LP, entitled *Pennies From...*

New Orleans/Dixieland trad jazz was not the only style to be found in the town at this time, however. Quality modern jazz could be heard at the Miller's Arms in Caversham during '74/'75 from such notable artists as Don Rendell and Dick Morrissey and, amazingly, the legendary tenor sax player Tubby Hayes (dubbed 'Europe's King Of Jazz') played at the club on de Montfort Island in May 1966, and also at Bulmershe College and the University within the next couple of years. The University had its own popular Jazz Club that drew big names, including the legendary American saxophonist Coleman Hawkins, British trumpeter Ian Carr and the sax player Sonny Rollins who, with drummer Max Roach and his band, were filmed for TV (see Chapter 3).

…and not forgetting Reading's Country Scene

In the early 70s Reading also had its own country music legend – Frank Jennings who, with his band The Syndicate, championed this style of music at a time when, like folk, it had not reached a mainstream audience. By 1975 a few pubs around the town were beginning to give this a go as they had folk, including the Lower Ship.

A great line-up of artists for Caversham Court Gardens in 1972

The latter years (1973–1976)

1973

The inflation that blighted the 70s began to bite hard and, as OPEC doubled the price of crude oil, it hit nearly 9%. Result? Strikes and a three-day week. Records got a lot thinner too. Nixon was removed from office in the US; at home, VAT was introduced and the UK decided to join the EEC. Meanwhile, the IRA stepped up their bombing campaign, with murderous results.

Glam rock dominated the singles charts, with Slade, Sweet, Suzi Quatro, Bowie and Gary Glitter all hitting the top spot, while American imports David Cassidy, The Jackson Five and those toothsome Osmonds (both individually and collectively) kept the teenyboppers happy. *Tubular Bells* continued to sell by the truckload, as did Elton John, Wings and Pink Floyd albums. Flares got wider and platforms higher, regardless of sex. Make-up for men became commonplace, especially at Bowie and Roxy Music shows. Status Quo gigs, on the other hand, attracted an audience clothed entirely in denim.

Around 20 concerts were staged at the Town Hall this year, ranging from the category-defying West Country combo Stackridge, who played twice, to the delightfully eccentric Henry Cow. This was the age of town hall gigs, and all bands conducting tours of the UK would have expected to be booked into a multitude of them, alongside universities and the odd specialist concert hall. There was still no need for elaborate security measures: music fans were unusually tolerant people who generally restricted themselves to a chorus of boos to signify displeasure. This would change as the music splintered, becoming increasingly diverse over the course of the decade – but you knew what you were signing up for when you bought a ticket to see Henry Cow!

While the mothership went from strength to strength, a double bill of bands featuring ex-Jethro Tull personnel appeared in January, both destined for relative obscurity. Having had a superb start with his post-Tull outfit Blodwyn Pig and an album packed full of great tunes back in 1969, it looked as if guitarist Mick Abrahams might run his old boss close in the commercial stakes; but it was not to be. Wild Turkey, the other band on the bill, were bassist Glen Cornick's project. This was a fine evening of music by two bands whose time was fast slipping away.

Status Quo played Reading twice this year: the Town Hall in March, and a career-defining appearance at the Festival in August that provided the track subsequently included on the live compilation album of the event. The release of the *Piledriver* album in December 1972 had consolidated the sound they had been working towards for a couple of years and set the pattern for their seemingly eternal career.

April also saw the return of Arthur Brown to his old stomping ground, his band Kingdom Come headlining a tour to promote his new album, *Journey*. Support came from French-boys Ange and turned out to be a revelation. Mike and Adrian were both present and impressed. Adrian recalls:

'Led by vocalist Christian Decamps, the band created a doom-laden, nightmarish storm of sound, a Brothers Grimm soundtrack of the darkest hue. Glove puppets featured in one song; Sooty and Sweep they were most definitely not! With the whole thing sung in French, this just added to the mystique as, being Brits, we had absolutely no idea what they were on about. It didn't happen often, but Arthur Brown was being upstaged.'

Adrian continues,

'Arthur's arrival on stage inside an enormous syringe, his body painted gold, began a recreation of the recently released platter that was almost perfect. With his rich baritone soaring and swooping across the material, his prolonged scream on the track 'Conception' chilled the sell-out crowds' blood. Telephones and three-headed fish made appearances courtesy of the road crew – it was that kind of an evening.'

The tragically overlooked but rather marvellous Skin Alley appeared in November. The previous year's marvellously packaged *Two Quid Deal* album was one of the best, full of intelligent, melodic songs played in a jazzy-progressive rock style that never outstayed its welcome.

Famously dismissed by 'Whispering' Bob Harris when he introduced the band on BBC2's *Old Grey Whistle Test* as 'not my sort of thing', in a live setting The Sensational Alex Harvey Band had few peers. The band exuded a sense of wickedness and excess unmatched

TOWN HALL, READING
CONCERT
MON., 26th NOVEMBER, '73 @ 8 p.m.
Admission **70p** incl. V.A.T.

№ 2 0 1

Doors Open 7.30 p.m.

in rock: their material was twisted and their humour positively evil. The band were in Reading touring to promote their second album, *Next*, released the same month as this show, November.

Gong closed the year at the Town Hall. Their appearance in December was part of a tour to promote the second instalment of an eventual trilogy of albums in their *Radio Gnome Invisible* series, fashioned around a mythical world of pot-headed pixies.

It was a good year for the Town Hall, but so too for the Top Rank, which could accommodate double the punters, either sitting on the floor or standing. Hit-makers Blackfoot Sue kicked off the new year there. They may only have had one big hit, but 'Standing in the Road' was a good one.

The University held a Rags gig at the Top Rank with headliners The Kinks in February. Augmented by the brass of former college favourites The Mike Cotton Sound they were re-emerging as a major live attraction on the college circuit, their student audience having been still in short pants during the band's hit-making heyday. However, with the legendary Sam & Dave appearing the following month, The

Drifters in June and the Chi-Lites and Detroit Emeralds in October, normal service for this venue resumed. Admission to the venue was often subject to compliance with a dress code (suspended for rock nights), which the publicity material went to some lengths to point out. Sadly, soul and R&B gigs tended to attract a different crowd. There was some crossover, but not much.

With glam rock dominating the singles charts, one of its biggest exponents, ex-Move and ELO founder Roy Wood's rock 'n' roll pranksters Wizzard, arrived in Reading in June. They had recently topped the charts with their second single and were to repeat the trick a couple of months later with 'Angel Fingers'. Hawkwind, meanwhile, whose double live album *Space Ritual* had been out since May, were on an upward trajectory. Having already outgrown the Town Hall, there was only the Top Rank left for the local promoter to consider. Dress code: patchouli oil and Afghans only. Hawkwind would headline Friday night at the Reading Festival the following year.

Live sounds, bands or just singers, were everywhere in the town, even in the old Abbey Gardens, but no venue promoted live acts as frequently as the Target. Most bands may not have been household names, but the pub was a valuable proving ground for young talent and could guarantee a decent crowd down there, especially on Fridays and Saturdays. By no means a large space, it made an audience of 50 sound like Wembley Arena. Old beat-boom hero Billy J. Kramer played the pub in May, although not with his old crew, The Dakotas. It had actually only been nine years since he last hit the top of the charts with the song 'Little Children', but it might just as well have been another lifetime. For Kramer, it would take a few years before the advent of the Solid Silver 60s Shows and chicken-in-the-basket venues provided regular employment again.

1974

With the three-day-week in full swing and power cuts becoming the norm, the year got off to a rather gloomy start from which it was slow to recover. Ted Heath narrowly lost the election and Harold Wilson returned, but inflation continued its rise and the country's economy slipped into the malaise with which the 70s are associated.

The Carpenters and their greatest hits collection topped the album charts for weeks, but there was also Bowie's *Diamond Dogs* album and continuing massive sales for *Tubular Bells, Dark Side of the Moon* and *Band on the Run*. TV gave us *Kojak, The Rockford Files* and an obsession with martial arts. The US series *Kung Fu* stoked the fires lit by Bruce Lee a couple of years earlier, and Carl Douglas had a massive hit with the somewhat gauche 'Kung Fu Fighting'.

Abba set out on the road to world domination by winning the Eurovision Song Contest, and Kraftwerk released the *Autobahn* album and headed off in an entirely different direction, laying the foundations for a new musical future in the process. The Bay City Rollers became massive both here and in the States.

The Rumble in the Jungle was probably the biggest sporting event of the year, with West Germany beating Cruyff's Holland in the World Cup Final a close second. Pocket calculators started to appear while Lord Lucan did the opposite. The IRA bombed pubs in Guildford and Birmingham with devastating effect, both physical and political.

Between them, Reading's premier venues, the Top Rank and the Town Hall, hosted around 50 live music promotions over the course of 1974, covering an extremely wide spectrum of music. But this is also true of the town generally: live music and formerly big stars popped up in some unlikely places. Long John Baldry, for example – mentor to Julie Driscoll and Rod Stewart as members of Steampacket, and a regular in dance halls and University Students' Unions throughout the 60s – could be found entertaining the punters at somewhere called Funkey's Dinateque on the Wokingham Road in October (although this seems an unnecessarily cruel fate for a former chart-topper).

The Upper Deck at the Lower Ship offered a selection of traditional jazz acts like Bernie Allen throughout the year, alongside country and western outfits such as Shucks and Country Fever. The Miller's Arms in Caversham continued to present jazz combos with modernist leanings like Edge, The Modern Jazz Sextet and The LMS Octet. Still going strong was the John Barleycorn Folk Club at the Wellington Arms with a full programme of floor singers and guests.

Just outside the town, the Falcon on the old Woodley aerodrome site decided to play host to a whole series of 1950s inspired rock 'n' roll combos with names straight out of the Larry Parnes stable of stars, such as Gale Fury and The Hurricanes. Half a mile away in Coronation Hall (reputedly a venue for early Rolling Stones rehearsals when Brian Jones had a girlfriend living nearby) our old friends Graphite provided the entertainment for an evening organised by the Worker's Revolutionary Party Young Socialists in late May.

Elsewhere local bands were still performing in church and village halls. You may have missed Sabannac Uriah at the Peppard Memorial Hall, which sounds like a rather heavy evening! Talking of heavy, even local public schools succumbed to the lure of rock 'n' roll, with Wellington College in Crowthorne booking UFO for a gig in June. The band were on the cusp of breaking big, having recruited eighteen-year-old German whizz-kid (and founder of metal legends The Scorpions) Michael Schenker the previous year.

Continuing with the heaviness for just a little longer, the Target continued offering a packed schedule of the up-and-coming throughout the year. Although it is difficult to find much information about bands like Magus, Oracle or Panic, the splendidly named Super Vole no doubt used their Target gig as a useful warm-up opportunity for their support slot for Stray at the legendary Roundhouse in London a couple of days later.

Ellis, who played in February and later that year at the long-since demolished Roundabout pub in Whitley, had serious pedigree: Steve Ellis had been the singer with 60s teeny-bop chart-topping favourites Love Affair. One might have expected the band at a larger venue.

Glam rock acts and soul music comprised the bulk of performances staged at the Top Rank over the year, with some notable rock performances thrown in, and country music represented by the Reading-based Frank Jennings Syndicate. Glam came in the shape of new boys Merlin, signed to CBS and due to do a nationwide tour supporting David Essex later in the year. Their star shone briefly and – frankly – not very brightly, in contrast to that of Alvin Stardust, who played in May, followed a few days later by The Glitter Band. The wonderful Suzi Quatro was booked by the University Rags Committee for their annual bash in the town, played wonderfully and lost them a small fortune. Finally, Mud arrived, having already scored three Top 10 hits this year, including 'Tiger Feet', which had hit the top spot in January.

The Climax Blues Band appeared in April and were in the process of gradually transforming themselves from being a rather dour but superior bunch of Chicago blues-loving lads from the Potteries into something a bit funkier. The enigmatic Medicine Head played in the same week. Six months earlier they had gone Top 10 with the song 'One and One is One'; they scored four Top 30 singles in total. Originally signed by DJ John Peel to his Dandelion label, they were a guitar/harmonica duo, to which the guitarist added percussion one-man-band-style.

The Top Rank will always be associated with providing a stage to some of the best US soul and R&B acts on tour in Europe, and 1974 was another vintage year in this respect. March saw performances by The Detroit Spinners and Limmie & Family Cookin', both acts with a hatful of recent Top 10 hits. In April the great Jimmie Ruffin hit the stage, his classic recording of 'What Becomes of the Broken Hearted' about to be re-released and climb to the number four slot. Consistent hit-makers The Stylistics played in May; the fact that they had nine Top 10 hits between 1972 and 1976 gives an idea of their pedigree.

Edwin Starr had become a Reading regular down the years, even touring the UK with members of one of the town's premier combos, The Memphis Gents, as his backing band back in the 60s. Here he was again at the Rank in June, this time sharing the gig with reggae superstar Jimmy Cliff. Talking of reggae superstars: the fabulous Toots & the Maytals made an appearance the same night as the annual Festival got under way. It would be another couple of years before the Marquee organisation was prepared to showcase reggae at the Reading Festival, and at this point reggae concerts and the Festival attracted radically different crowds.

The fabulous Equals appeared at the Town Hall in June, supported by an old Reading dance hall favourite, Jimmy James. Although main man Eddy Grant had departed in 1971 with some serious health issues, The Equals were always a class act, with or without Grant, and one can only assume the chairs were removed from the hall for this particular evening as no one was going to remain seated for long. Their multi-racial line-up was radical for a British hit-making band in 1968, with only The Foundations sharing that honour on this side of the pond. Thank goodness for progress.

Leo Sayer's January's concert at the Town Hall, a month after his first number two, 'The Show Must Go On', was a total sell-out, though ticketless and tearful teenagers (some so young that they were escorted by their mums and dads) queued for hundreds of yards through the town after a mix-up that suggested tickets were available on the door. Sayer also played the Rank at the end of the year.

Hot on the heels of their one and only UK hit, 'Radar Love', Dutch band Golden Earring turned up at the Town Hall, with support from fellow countrymen Alquin. They were using The Who's quadrophonic sound system, being label-mates of theirs and support act on their up-coming tour, so at the very least they would have made quite a racket. Old favourites Savoy Brown, the Edgar Broughton Band and Stray played the venue over the year, their UK appeal gradually becoming more 'selective' (as Spinal Tap might say). Also, Gallagher & Lyle (the songwriting heart of McGuinness Flint) played in September; they had a couple of Top 10 hits 18 months later before being overwhelmed by the punk tsunami.

The Syd Lawrence Orchestra were regular Town Hall stars and appeared twice in 1974, perfectly recreating Glen Millers' unique sound, spot-on for dancing or just tapping your toes, proving that Reading boasted a music scene for all ages.

1975

Top selling album releases this year included Led Zeppelin's *Physical Graffiti* and Pink Floyd's *Wish You Were Here*. Queen's album *A Night at the Opera* propelled the band into the big league, and Elton John, Wings and Rod Stewart continued to release chart-topping albums. Bowie's *Young Americans* LP enhanced his chameleon career further, and his re-released 'Space Oddity' single topped the charts towards the year's end. Elsewhere, ominously but unnoticed, The Sex Pistols played their first gig at Saint Martin's College in London.

The Moorgate tube disaster left 43 dead, Margaret Thatcher became leader of the Conservative Party, and press allegations about Jeremy Thorpe began to intensify. Peter Benchley's book *Jaws* had already been in the best-seller lists for over a year when the release of Spielberg's film created the cinematic event of the year – Kung Fu was out, sharks were in. Saigon fell to the North Vietnamese army and the war ended, prompting much hand-wringing and soul-searching in the US for a generation. In Cambodia, the Khmer Rouge set about murdering their own citizens on a scale not seen since the Holocaust. The English landscape was being devastated by something called

Dutch Elm Disease: millions of trees died across the nation, changing forever the landscape depicted by Constable and Gainsborough.

Reading Festival attracted serious national coverage when the town was overwhelmed by an estimated 30,000 extra people who arrived *sans* tickets, drawn by the progressive rock band Yes and proving that talk of the genre's fading appeal was somewhat premature. The Festival organisation sold them tickets and let them in under pressure from the police (and in fear of a repeat of the Viking invasions of the 9th century). Otherwise, the year in Reading was relatively low-key, musically.

For many of us young people a night out meant finding a venue where live music was playing. Reading's colleges and university could usually be relied upon to have something going on, especially at weekends, and 1975 was no exception. However, if one of your group of friends happened to have a car, then the world was your oyster, as they say. And you didn't need to go too far either – which was just as well for five hulking lads packed into a Mini.

Among the smaller venues situated within easy driving distance, the Nag's Head in High Wycombe was probably without equal. Run since 1968 by the estimable Ron Watts, it had in previous years booked artists of the calibre of Muddy Waters, Howlin' Wolf and John Lee Hooker into an upstairs bar that held 300 at an absolute push. In 1975 Watts took on a further promotional opportunity at the Crown in Marlow and pointed the way to the future by presenting proto-punks Eddie and the Hot Rods there in October.

If it was a Friday, then the chances were that Wokingham Rock Club would have something on, usually by a group of local lads, like Greek Street or Night Porter, just starting out. The club handed them the opportunity to play in front of a live audience in decent surroundings, and the idea worked well for a couple of years: fair play to those who ran it.

The premier venue in the area, however, certainly as far as rock fans were concerned, was Bracknell Sports Centre, a venue that had played host to Slade at their peak, Roxy Music, Free, and even the great Captain Beefheart. Most of us fans were unconcerned about the environment in which we indulged our passion (the size of the PA being our main concern). This was just as well as the Sports Centre was no more than a featureless barn with a stage at one end. There was a bar, however, and because of its cavernous capacity you could turn up ticketless and were almost guaranteed admission.

Hawkwind kicked off the year for the Sports Centre (they played the venue a total of five times over the 70s and 80s). American Southern rock exponents Black Oak Arkansas played in February and Gong in April. Thin Lizzy's appearance coincided with the start of what is now regarded as their classic era, signalled by the release of their fifth album, *Fighting* – twin guitars pouring forth molten gold. Back Street Crawler's appearance in October had to be cancelled, due to their guitarist, former Free man Paul Kossoff, having been rushed to hospital with an 'unknown illness'. This is likely to have been a heroin overdose, an addiction that would lead to his death on a plane some five months later.

Maybe the Top Rank was closed for a refit this year; in any case research suggests there were only two shows advertised, The Chi-Lites in February and those Hawkwind boys again in December. In between these dates? No idea. Perhaps management just cut down on advertising costs.

The Town Hall, on the other hand, played host to at least a show per month, starting with South Wales heroes Budgie. Their intentionally sparsely arranged heaviness helped define metal in its early days. The year saw the return to the Hall of Rory Gallagher, Barclay James Harvest, Stackridge, Fruupp, Syd Lawrence and those Pink Fairies again. The band had reconvened at the Roundhouse back in July, reuniting the original line-up and adding Larry Wallis, Paul Rudolf's replacement, but it didn't last. Things seldom did with The Fairies, the ultimate anarcho-hippy combo.

One of the most curious bookings at the Hall concerned the band Love Affair, which – after many a line-up change since its inception in 1966 – had split in 1973. The original drummer, Maurice Bacon, had taken over the management and recruited a band to play under the Love Affair moniker (neither the first nor the last time for this kind of thing to be done – remember that Velvet Underground gig at the Top Rank in 1972?). This incarnation of Love Affair toured the UK and the Continent for 15 months before breaking up.

Camel closed the year at the Town Hall; it was the last night of their *Snow Goose* tour. They played the whole of the album and most of their previous release, *Mirage*, as well. Attendee James Carter take up the story.

Keen photographer Adrian Moulton took this picture in Reading in 1976

'Forty-five years on, this still ranks as one of my best gigs ever. This was gentle, melody-based prog, but live, Camel had a real urgency and energy and, being the end of the tour, they had become a well-oiled machine. We hung around afterwards and the band were most amenable, offering us drumsticks and plectrums as souvenirs, and beers. Ten minutes in, the roadies turned up, setting off fire-extinguishers on all and sundry; a customary end-of-tour gag, apparently.'

Of the smaller venues across the town the Wellington Arms in Whitley Street was still flying the flag for a town-based folk club under the John Barleycorn moniker, and the Miller's Arms in Caversham did the same for jazz, hosting British jazz heavyweights Dick Morrissey and Don Rendell in the early months of the year. Country music still featured at the Upper Deck at the Lower Ship, and the British Legion in Tilehurst played host to Arkansas-born country boy Vernon Oxford, who was in the throes of re-launching his career in the UK.

The Merry Maidens pub on the Shinfield Road always had a reputation for being somewhat prone to trouble; it was the kind of place that would fall ominously silent when a stranger entered. In this period they often booked former 1960s bands who had enjoyed one spectacular success, such as The Applejacks (in May) and Plastic Penny (in July). There was a market for this in the area: the Henwick in Thatcham offered similar fare, perhaps slightly rockier, with Ace and The Equals, among others.

The Target was busy as usual, featuring established acts like Ron Watts' own Cajun-influenced perennial support act Brewer's Droop and London pub favourites Red Beans & Rice, as well as a long list of others, some with the dullest band names in music history: Impulse, Wisper, Wheels, Farm, Kav, Factory. Still – at the end of November some lot called The Stranglers turned up.

1976

In another year scarred by the troubles in Northern Ireland, the IRA brought the conflict into the heart of London. A heatwave scorched the country bare for three months of the summer; the drought, somewhat inevitably, only came to an end during the Reading Festival. Prime Minister Wilson resigned, and James Callaghan began his stint as PM, a tenure that coincided with Britain's continued economic decline and seemingly endless industrial conflict. There was pride, however, in the first commercial flights of Concorde, and for the next 25 years it was possible to set your watch by the aircraft's late morning pass of Reading, bound for New York. You could certainly hear it!

In April Brotherhood of Man won the Eurovision Song Contest for the UK; they were no Abba. In October British Rail introduced the InterCity 125, shortening the journey time from Reading to London considerably.

With the England cricket team getting thrashed by the West Indies, it was the perfect time for reggae to begin its commercial break-through, aided by Virgin Records' 69p compilation *The Front Line*. 'Hotel California' by The Eagles was everywhere, as was *Frampton Comes Alive!* and Stevie Wonder's *Songs in the Key of Life*. Hugely successful releases by Boston and Thin Lizzy gave encouragement to the old rock order of things, but the year also saw the release of first albums by Blondie and The Ramones. With disco music becoming ever more prominent in the charts, it was the pure pop of Abba that held sway, hitting the top spot three times.

The Sex Pistols' May appearance at Reading University may only have been witnessed by a mere handful, but then there was the Bill Grundy episode in December, and then... – there it was, creeping into the Top 30 at number 27 for the final chart of the year: 'Anarchy in the UK'.

After a run of spectacular presentations at the Town Hall over the previous five years, suddenly they ceased. There were but four evenings booked in 1976 for what could loosely be described as rock concerts, and two of those were cancelled. Perhaps the price for a booking had massively increased or – more likely – the local authorities were becoming increasingly concerned about sound levels at concerts. One of the handful of promotions attempted that year was a double-header pitting Boxer against Widowmaker in March, but with all eyes firmly fixed on the lure of the Yankee dollar they both managed to produce music that was not just undemanding, but dull and predictable with it. Budgie returned in May, promoting their new LP, *If I Were Brittania I'd Waive The Rules*, and Prelude played in early June. They were a vocal group who had scored a minor hit on both sides of the Atlantic with an *a cappella* version of Neil Young's 'After The Goldrush' and went on to further success in the 80s. It is highly unlikely there were problems with decibel levels on this occasion.

AC/DC were over in the UK for the first time trying to make a breakthrough, though their support slot on the Back Street Crawler tour was scuppered due to Paul Kossoff's untimely demise. Derided by journalists for being musical Neanderthals, they were nonetheless making quite an impression, massively enhanced by an appearance at the Reading Festival later this year. Destined to become one of the most successful and enduring rock bands on the planet, they were to return to Reading the following summer. James Carter witnessed their Top Rank show:

'Angus Young did this bit where he jumped into the audience and fell on his back, writhing around on the floor still playing excellent guitar. When he came to get up, he fell backwards onto me. I reached out to support him and had the privilege of briefly touching his topless and sweaty back.'

Ugh!

In contrast to the Town Hall, the Top Rank ran a full programme of events throughout the year. In February a financially disastrous presentation by the University Rags Committee featured Showaddywaddy, who attracted a reasonable turn-out, apparently, but only half of that required to break even, let alone make a profit for the designated charities. The rest of the year saw a somewhat desultory smattering of rock acts on offer, the rather underwhelming Woody Woodmansey's U Boat in August being one of them.

Former pub-rockers Dr Feelgood were riding high in the album charts with their third album, *Stupidity*, a live set recorded the previous year, when they played a sell-out show at the Rank in October. For the rest of the year at the Rank, it was a full house of the best American soul, R&B and disco acts around. The Fatback Band played twice, the first time in February as their single 'Spanish Hustle' went Top 10. The Miracles and The Drifters followed in the early summer, the former having charted with 'Love Machine' in January and the latter having been rarely out of the charts since the early 70s. Their music is as popular today as it ever was, unashamedly undemanding and upbeat and oblivious to any changes in fashion. Kool and the Gang played in June; already big stars in the States, it would be another couple of years before their hard work paid off on this side of the Atlantic. Liverpool's own soul sensation The Real Thing arrived in September of what had become their break-through year. They had hit the top spot in June with 'You To Me Are Everything', and this month saw the follow-up, 'Can't Get By Without You', reach number two. Johnny 'Guitar' Watson and The Chi-Lites made return visits, and reggae star Tito Simon, who'd had a minor hit the previous year with 'This Monday Morning Feeling', made an appearance. And then there was the mighty War, who had long parted company with ex-Animals singer Eric Burdon and charted with the track 'Low Rider' early in the year. Destined to be danced to for the rest of eternity, this track alone would mark out this multi-ethnic band as something special, but there were many, many others.

The smaller pubs and clubs around town were busy pulling in the punters with their own, individual take on the music scene. The Miller's Arms was still presenting the best in modern jazz, including the likes of Lennie Best, Don Rendell and Stan Tracey, and the John Barleycorn Folk Club at the Wellington Arms was still going strong.

After successes the previous year, the British Legion in Tilehurst decided to set up a dedicated Country and Western Music Club, and the Merry Maidens continued the cabaret/showbiz format that had been so successful the previous year. The emphasis was firmly on dancing, as it was at the Thing-A-Me-Jig Club, soon to be known as Harvey Wallbangers, so what they thought of Clayson and the Argonauts' gig in May of that year is anyone's guess, because a dance band they certainly were not. Alan Clayson had a demanding stage presence, and with his excellent band giving shape to his unique material, he could, on a good night, sweep all before him. After all, who else was weaving tragic tales of the Dark Ages with songs like 'Pagan Mercia'?

The Target featured the likes of east-London rockers Slowbone. Some bands who played have left a mark down the years, but most haven't – whatever happened to the wonderfully named Swift Whippet one wonders? At the edge of town, the Calcot Hotel was establishing itself as an early example of the unfairly-derided chicken-in-a-basket type of venue, offering a basic menu to be consumed to the sounds of 60s chart-toppers The Tremeloes or The Foundations. The Henwick in Thatcham ran a similar operation, hosting Dave Berry and the Cruisers in June, a hugely successful artist in the 60s for whom Alan Clayson provided some material in the 80s.

And beyond? The American airbase at Greenham Common was obviously trying to improve its public image by advertising on-camp gigs to the local populace. Old dance hall favourite Geno Washington was booked, as were James and Bobby Purify. The usual array of top-notch bands came to Bracknell Sports Centre, including The Sensational Alex Harvey Band, ex-Family boys Streetwalkers, Hawkwind (almost inevitably), and those rapidly rising stars, Thin Lizzy. Oh, and Disco-Tex & His Sex-O-Lettes. The town was also hosting a successful jazz festival in July, an event that ran annually until the mid-80s, while Whitehouse Farm in Spencer's Wood staged a three-day event entitled The Berkshire Midsummer Folk Festival. Wokingham Rock Club was still going strong, although rather ominously the name had been amended to the Wokingham Heavy Rock Club.

Finally, something of a curiosity. Towards the end of June, Ashmead Hall hosted a performance by a band called Nan Carey's Wood. This was a personal project for Nettlebed resident Kenny Lynch, a highly successful singer and songwriter both for films and the likes of The Small Faces, among many others. He was one of the first black faces to regularly star on British TV. Growing frustrated with being classed as a cabaret singer, he fancied his chances in rock. He gathered a team of top-notch local players, named them after a haunted wood near his home and wrote most of their country-tinged material. It was a short-lived dream; this concert was one of only a handful for the band, and Lynch soon returned to the celebrity golf circuit. No chance of a reunion, sadly, as this highly talented trailblazer died at the end of 2019.

Nan Carey's Wood featuring Kenny Lynch (third from left) in 1976

Reading University 1973–1976

Both The Who and The Doors were huge international names at the time the University managed to secure their services. Not so Lou Reed: his first post-Velvet Underground album had not exactly been a triumph, but his second, *Transformer*, was a game-changer. A glam rock milestone, it also featured the single 'Walk on the Wild Side', which went Top 10 in the UK in May 1973. Good news for Mr Reed and for music generally, not so good for the University: Reed pulled out when far more lucrative offers were suddenly forthcoming. Shame – it would have been a memorable event.

Other cancellations in the first part of the year included Soft Machine and Barclay James Harvest. The latter were shocked by the protests and bomb scares at the universities of Leeds and Hull and were no doubt mulling over the wisdom of having played some gigs in apartheid-era South Africa. Agencies had university social secretaries over a barrel, it seems: no doubt the contracts signed by all parties included some extremely small print.

On the plus side, British guitar legend Jeff Beck's short-lived trio with ex-Vanilla Fudge members Tim Bogert and Carmine Appice went down extremely well, encoring with snatches of old Beatles and Yardbirds numbers. Supported by ex-Yes axeman Tony Bank's band Flash, this was an evening of the finest 70s guitar overload. In a similar vein, the Wishbone Ash gig in the spring was both a sell-out and a triumph, with hundreds sitting outside on the grass catching the vibe of a band at its finest. Adrian Whittaker in *Shell* remarked, 'Having played two encores, the band didn't stick around [and left] the audience recovering from what, in my opinion, was the best gig we've seen here this year'. But you can judge for yourself, as four of the tracks on their album *Live Dates* were recorded on that night.

Enjoying an Indian summer, The Kinks played a Rags event at the Top Rank back in February; their two recent albums, *Muswell Hillbillies* and *Celluloid Heroes*, had been enthusiastically received, so one of the greatest UK bands of the 60s was back and going down a treat in Reading.

1974 saw the return to the Union Hall of University favourite Al Stewart playing tracks from his new album *Past, Present and Future*, with a band featuring ex-Curved Air keyboard player Francis Monkman. Rags booked glam rock queen Suzi Quatro for the annual

Top Rank slot but lost a lot of money on the venture, and progressive rock originals Procol Harum played the Union Hall, encoring with the inevitable 'Whiter Shade of Pale'. Prog may have originated in the UK, but Europeans too produced some quality performers, the University taking a punt on a fair few of them. Irish band Fruupp pleasantly creamed classical and folk music into a light sponge fairy-cake and appeared in May, as did Italians P.F.M., whose musical con-coction was flashier and jazzier. Anglo-French stoners Gong, rapidly turning from being the pot-head pixies of yore into the jazz-rock immortals, came down to earth to play the Union Hall in October.

Best of all were Magma, a French band led by drummer Christian Vander. Promoting their third album *Mekanic Destruktiv Kommandoh,* they performed this intimidating work in full. Adrian Moulton re-ports, 'With the band (all twelve of them) dressed in black and Vander behind his kit centre-stage an utterly mesmerising figure, they produced a hypnotic, constantly driving rhythm of sub-operatic hyper-intensity that held the audience spell-bound.'

With a student body far larger than Reading's two other colleges combined, and various halls of residence all wanting to stage their own entertainments across the academic calendar, it is no wonder that the musical events staged within the University tend to domi-nate this review. Both Reading Technical College and Bulmershe College had healthy scenes of their own, and from 1974 onwards probably better reflected the changing musical landscape of the country as a whole. They had smaller budgets too, so no chance of booking the likes of The Who, even if they did have a space big enough to stage them. As fellow NUS members, their students could attend University events, and there was a degree of co-operation during Rag Week when the two colleges would stage musical fund-raising events to contribute to the whole, but they were always the junior partners. There was downright snobbery too: University alum-ni tending to view College students the way Londoners regard people living north of Watford.

On the 18 of October 1974 Reading Tech staged emerging rock leg-ends and darlings of the burgeoning London pub scene, Dr Feelgood. This gig was a real coup for the social secretary – this was the band that prepared the ground for the acceptance of punk rock 18 months later. They were a reminder of where British pop music had emerged from more than ten years previously, when bands like The Rolling Stones and The Animals attempted to copy black American styles and inadvertently created rock.

March the following year saw the band play a rammed Bridges Hall at Bulmershe College. If they, like their pub-rock contemporaries, were a throwback to the dawn of rock, so was the fact that everyone was on their feet from the start, working up a lather of frenzied sweat and going back to digs happy. The College social secretaries had learned the lesson preached by their opposite numbers in the University halls of residence when they had booked the likes of Osibisa and Shakin' Stevens and the Sunsets in previous years: it's the weekend, and students just wanna have some fun.

Things had come full circle since Pink Floyd's appearance in the Great Hall back in early 1967, when audiences began to sit cross-legged, the better to 'get into' the experience. The London pub-rock scene transferred easily to the college circuit, was affordable and guaranteed a good time. Between 1974 and 1976 Bulmershe hosted, among others, Afro-jazzers Zzebra, the funk and soul of Kokomo and Cado Belle, the Latin beats of Gonzalez, Joe Strummer's 101ers, Ian Dury's Kilburn and the High Roads, Kursaal Flyers, the rock 'n' roll of Mickey Jupp and Shakin' Stevens, and the soon-to-be-huge Graham Parker & the Rumour.

There was also Reading's own Gerald T. Moore, better known then as G.T. Moore, along with his Reggae Guitars. Skins, mods and working-class kids had been hip to the beats emanating from Jamaica for a decade or more, but it took a man like Moore to achieve the breakthrough with white, middle-class rock crowds. The previous summer The Reggae Guitars had played to a 50,000-plus crowd in Hyde Park in a gig headlined by prog heroes Kevin Ayers and Gong and had gone down a storm. Enlisting the recording engineer who had worked with Bob Marley on his album *Burnin',* and former Free man and Wailer session player Rabbit Bundrik on additional keyboards, G.T. Moore & The Reggae Guitars' first album was a triumph, capturing that laid-back Jamaican vibe in a studio in downtown Woking.

Bridges Hall was again packed with students grooving to the irresistible rhythms of The Reggae Guitars, and the pioneering Moore once again able to soak up the adulation of a home-town crowd. Within a year we had all bought the Virgin Records budget sampler

The Front Line, Marley's *Live at the Lyceum* was released, and three reggae acts appeared at the 1976 Reading Festival. The Reggae Guitars had played no small part in this breakthrough.

To some extent it was business as usual at the University through 1975. The visit of glam-rock legends Sparks at the end of the previous year had been a high-point, but Curved Air seemed a rather tame choice, and Argent, according to Peter Carr in *Shell*, were well past their sell-by date: 'If Rod Argent looked uncomfortable, he'd every goddam right to be. Because right now Argent are a band drifting aimlessly.'

Ex-Small Faces Ronnie Lane and his band Slim Chance played the Rag Ball, the three albums they recorded of good-time English country music now regarded as minor classics; and the classy, but often drunk, John Martyn played the Union Hall.

The year 1976 did not get off to a good start. Dutch prog wizards Focus turned up minus ace guitarist Jan Akkerman, who had quit a matter of days previously. His severely under-rehearsed replacement struggled, as did the band. Booking Showaddywaddy for the annual Rags event at the Top Rank proved a financial disaster, but at least Mud sold out the Union Hall.

The University seemed to have got into the habit of booking acts that were, frankly, trading on someone else's reputation. Jack the Lad went down well, despite being the half of Lindisfarne without the tunes, and the Rag Ball featured Bowie's backing band, The Spiders from Mars. Mott came along in March; they used to be Mott the Hoople, but their main man Ian Hunter was long gone.

Al Stewart turned up again in the autumn, promoting his excellent *Year of the Cat* album, as did ex-Amen Corner and solo hit-maker Andy Fairweather-Lowe. New Zealand art-rockers Split Enz took a support slot in October. It would be a few years and a radical toning down of their image before they hit the charts with 'I Got You', recording a run of superlative albums and eventually morphing into Crowded House. Pub rockers like Roogalator started to appear in the schedules, as did so-called new-wave bands like The Doctors of Madness and, almost unnoticed, The Sex Pistols.

The band were booked by Fine Art department student Richard Boon (soon to be manager of Manchester's finest, Buzzcocks) on the premise that – placed in an art studio – they could be considered 'performance art' and contribute to his final degree marks. Although articles had started to appear about the band in the music press (including reports of a punch-up at the Nashville Rooms in West London a week prior to the Reading gig), the word was not yet out. The Ramones' first album had only just been released, and the notorious Bill Grundy interview was some six months away. You would have had to have your ear close to the ground to have picked up on the quartet's Vivienne-Westwood-attired notoriety as they hadn't been near a recording studio at this point.

Fair play to Boon then; but the Fine Art department had form. A few years earlier a mostly female musical and performance collective centred on the department and going under the name of Moodies had scooped up lumps of Weimar Berlin and Warhol's 60s New York – all leopard-skin tops, PVC minis and heavy make-up – and presented it with a flamboyant, studied disregard for musical accuracy. Fellow Reading student Andy Mackay, a founder member of Roxy Music, was impressed, as was *Rocky Horror Show* creator Richard O'Brien. They were featured in the *Sunday Times Magazine* and were, perhaps not surprisingly, very popular in Germany.

About 20 people paid 50 pence to see The Sex Pistols. John Lydon greeted the gathering with a neat put-down: 'Art students? We've seen your paintings. Is this what we pay our taxes for?' According to Chris Godfrey, the band 'played well enough and were nowhere near as shoddy as the press had led people to believe. I was expecting Woolworth's guitars and crap amps.' They would go on to confound most people's expectations – and not just those of middle-class students looking for a bit of controversy – by going on to record one of the finest rock albums of all time just one year later.

The Reading Festival

The (11th)* National Jazz, Blues and Rock Festival, 25–27 June 1971

Organised by London's legendary Marquee Club in conjunction with the National Jazz Federation, the inaugural Reading event was planned as just one part of a wider 'Festival of Reading' that was being held to celebrate two seminal events in the town's history: the founding of Reading Abbey 850 years previously, and the first mention of the town in the Anglo-Saxon Chronicle in the year 871, when it was under attack from Viking raiders.

'Chirpy Chirpy, Cheep Cheep' by Middle of the Road was the number one single in the UK in June 1971, but the local press scaremongering leading up to the Festival was notably much less chirpy – more akin to warnings of another Viking invasion! Residents were told to lock their sheds, take in the milk and leave no money for tradesmen on the doorsteps. One report in the *Reading Chronicle* told of 'barricades around properties near the Thames, with guard dogs, security patrols and padlocks being employed as a safeguard against marauding pop fans.'

The Caversham Bridge Hotel immediately adjacent to the site, where many of the Thames Valley police officers were staying, was also getting ready: 'We are preparing for the worst. [...] we will not be serving them [the pop fans] drinks. The hotel will be open for meals, but pop fans who look like pop fans will not be served'. There seemed to be real animosity against the Festival: 'Prejudice Against Pop Festival Say Organisers' was the headline in the *Chronicle* on 21 May. Leading up to the big weekend at least the weather forecast was looking promising. Wrong!

'Reading: Washed Out' and 'Singing in the Rain' were just two of the headlines that appeared in *Melody Maker's* report of the 1971 Festival. Roy Hollingworth added, somewhat depressingly,

---

* The 11th festival was not numbered on posters and advertising, which led to incorrect numbering of the festivals in the following two years. The error was not corrected until 1974, the year of the 14th festival.

'One always recalls sepia prints of Somme or Verdun when humans bog in mud and vehicles plough up filth and everything sinks in the floodlit flecks of thick rain. There was this flautist from Warm Dust, standing at the prow of the stage, the rain lashing into him. Water ran down his hair, down nose and chin, changed direction when it hit the flute and drained from the musician by using the instrument as guttering. And music still came out...'

Despite the inclement weather conditions, further reports from the front-line trenches by Roy Carr and James Johnson of the *New Musical Express* were more upbeat. Their reception of the up-and-coming bands traditionally showcased by the National Jazz, Blues and Rock Festival could raise some bands' profiles significantly; this year they highlighted Wishbone Ash, Lindisfarne, Van Der Graaf Generator, Bell and Arc, Demick & Armstrong and, in particular, Medicine Head. From the already more established acts it was Rory Gallagher and Americans Sha Na Na who 'stole the entire weekend.'

Universe (which featured Olly Alcock) playing the Reading Festival in 1971. Confusingly another band of the same name were around at roughly the same time.

In addition, Arthur Brown with his band Kingdom Come provided what James Johnson called 'the most amazing spectacle of the festival.' The set began with Arthur hanging from a wooden cross and became stranger as it went on. Health and safety had yet to be invented: flares and smoke bombs exploded, then a bonfire was lit, and Arthur, screaming his agonised vocals, jumped off stage and into the audience before climbing up the scaffolding. As the band created an uneasy atmosphere to complement the theatrics, the crowd became so enthusiastic that at the end they invaded stage, a minor riot ensued and chaos reigned.

When the Festival had finished and the mud was drying out, the post-mortem began. There were reports that the event had bombed and been a financial failure. According to Festival director Brian Sommerville, this was totally untrue: 'Very pleasant festival indeed. About 15–18,000 people were present, and the bands had the crowd often on their feet.'

The *Reading Chronicle* also reported a decidedly mixed reaction to the weekend's events. Under the headline 'Pop Festival Boost for Caversham Traders' it noted that the shopkeepers 'would back the suggestion of having another pop festival next year'. If the shopkeepers were happy, others clearly weren't. 'The fans, however, are not keen to return,' the *Chronicle* continued, 'many left bitter about the event with complaints about high prices on the site, the lack of good food, shelter and drinking water and a poor sound system.' One of them, John May from London, said, 'The ground was waterlogged, and the police were breathing down our necks!'

Despite all these issues, rumours and denials, history shows that this was the beginning of something special. The fans would indeed return; local traders, as well as the organisers and the local Council, would continue to rake in the cash; and the Festival would evolve into one of the music calendar's major annual events.

For the end of June, Friday was a pretty gloomy, grey day, and chilly. Island signings Clouds were playing as my girlfriend Jennie and I settled ourselves down among the crowd. I remember them being kind of OK, utilising a few tricks such as the drummer bashing out rhythms with his sticks on the bass guitar. But hey – first band, first Festival. They went down well, and we had the rest of a chilly day to enjoy.

The legendary Glastonbury Fayre had been staged the previous week and many people had travelled from there to Reading, bringing an entirely different festival philosophy with them. Within a couple of hours of arriving we were handed a spirit-duplicated flyer (remember them?) informing us that we should rise up and take control of this capitalist shithole and tear down the fences. There weren't many takers. The toilets were adequate, food stalls kind of OK, and most of the police were outside the arena, although admittedly giving a good many longhairs the third degree regarding drug possession.

Armada, Daddy Longlegs and hotly tipped Charisma-signed artists Bell and Arc came and went. Finally, Friday night headliners Kingdom Come hit us full-on. With three flaming crosses erected in front of the stage, Arthur Brown appeared through the smoke and the noise, stripped to the waist and face demonically painted, to gyrate in his unique and unsettling way to the killer riff that opens the *Galactic Zoo Dossier* album. To say that I was transfixed would be an understatement. This was a freak show, a circus for the rock generation, with Arthur as a demonic Master of Ceremonies howling and screeching his way through the entire spectacular album. Costumes changed, characters appeared from the wings in outlandish guise, Arthur disappeared for ten minutes – allowing the superb band to demonstrate just how much fun prog could be – and then reappeared, his 6ft 4in frame wrapped in a cloak adorned with the moon and stars. Quite an end to the first day at the first Reading Festival, and it was rather fitting that an ex-Reading student had started this fire.

The ride into Reading down the Caversham Road on my trusty Lambretta on day two revealed a scene that has been recreated every year since. Hordes of hairy, denim-clad punters were alighting at the station and heading for the Richfield Avenue campsites, past a multitude heading in the other direction, somewhat grimier and dishevelled, seeking town-centre supermarkets to stock up on beer and instant noodles. All along the road, stalls had sprung up selling everything from hamburgers to Indian jewellery, with local shops cashing in on the bonanza.

Charisma-signed band Audience is one of the few acts that I remember from that grey, chilly June afternoon. Highlighting much of the material from their recently released album *House on the Hill*, they were strong on melody, with singer Howard Werth's powerful vocals cutting through the phasing of sound caused by the strong winds.

Lindisfarne's performance was a breakthrough for the band. Packed full of stoner Geordie cheer, they got a standing ovation from the shivering crowd. Their near-perfect blend of stand-out tunes, intelligent lyrics, intricate harmonies, interweaving mandolin, violin and acoustic guitar arrangements and witty stage banter won a host of new fans on this day. Closing number 'We Can Swing Together', a story of a north-east drugs bust, resonated with a crowd that felt harassed by the overactive operation of the local police force.

I only made a fleeting visit to the site on Sunday. I caught the last number of Transatlantic act CMU as I made my way to the exit, and it was enough to make me stop and watch. Impressive, I thought. The following year they released their second and final album, *Space Cabaret*, which remains a largely undiscovered prog gem.

The weather hadn't been too kind, and neither had the police. It was muddy, cold and, with some notable exceptions, musically rather conservative and low-key. But it had been a success. The hippies hadn't rioted; Reading wasn't awash with immorality; and thanks to Harold Pendleton's Marquee organisation the town was now firmly on the rock radar of the nation, where it has remained ever since.

Adrian Moulton

The 11th (actually the 12th) National Jazz, Blues and Rock Festival, 11–13 August 1972

In the lead-up to the Festival in 1972 the people of Reading seem to have been generally more welcoming, compared with the previous year. After all, the Festival turned out to have quite a few positive aspects, not least the effect on the local economy, with many traders and publicans making fistfuls of cash. According to the Chief Constable of Thames Valley Police,

'Few crimes were reported throughout the period of the 1971 festival and no crimes of violence occurred within the festival site. It is significant that whereas a number of general complaints had been received from local residents prior to the staging of the 1971 festival, not one letter of complaint or concern was expressed from residents in the area prior to the 1972 festival.'

However, the performance of Thames Valley's finest was once again in the headlines, with no respite from the previous year's heavy, aggressive tactics. They made scores of arrests, this time with the added provocation of the sight and noise of their helicopter, a near-constant feature in the sky above the banks of the Thames, dampening the whole atmosphere, hassling and unnerving mostly peaceful festival-goers.

Due to a significant upgrade of the festival sound equipment, numerous complaints were made about heavy rock music audible through windows and waking up dogs and children. In fact, according to one local paper, 'The full force of the gigantic sound system was heard all over West Reading,' which particularly affected patients at the then nearby Battle Hospital, adding fuel to a strengthening opposition to the Festival.

This bad feeling was echoed by the manager of the adjacent Caversham Bridge Hotel, who had spent £600 (around £3500 in today's money) erecting a fence around the entire building to keep out the great unwashed, or 'parasites', as another local resident called them. He told the *Reading Chronicle*, 'I have at least 600 reasons that the festival should not be held on the same site next year,' and suggested the event be moved across town to Palmer Park in future.

On a more positive note, conditions on site were certainly better than they had been the previous year, helped by mainly good weather. The police reported few incidents, saying that there were more problems at the nearby Knowl Hill Steam Rally! Many residents in the town felt that soccer hooliganism was much more of a problem.

'A good festival and the best of the year so far,' was the verdict of *Sounds* reporter Ray Telford in his write-up for the year, although in the same pages a couple of his colleagues were less kind, reporting that not many bands, 'did anything very startling'. The *Melody Maker* hacks almost gushed that Saturday's performances were in the main excellent, with the weekend's highlights being Genesis on Friday, then Focus, Edgar Broughton, Jonathan Kelly, Johnny Otis and The Faces on the Saturday. Sunday's honours went to Stackridge, Vinegar Joe and headliners Ten Years After.

Once the dust had settled, the 1972 Festival was deemed a success; the organisers declared it a hit and even confirmed that the event had made a modest profit. All of this must have made for sweet music to the ears of the organisers, Marquee and the NJF, after the negative fallout of the previous year, and they would have been further encouraged by the *Evening Post*'s final headline, which wondered if there would now be 'A rocking Reading every year?'

A ticket to the 1972 Festival that's (almost) survived intact!

I caught the train back from a very soggy camping holiday in North Wales with my wife Jennie, five-months pregnant at the time, to attend the 1972 event, even though she'd had quite enough of surviving under canvas in inclement weather. With the Festival edging towards its long-term August Bank Holiday date, the weather proved to be a great deal better than the previous year, although still damn cold at night. We managed a couple of days, packing up on the Sunday morning and making it home for much-needed baths.

I can only recall two or three bands from Friday, but my memories are clearer of the Saturday, which brought The Johnny Otis Show to the stage, complete with the unforgettable Three Tons of Joy, his backing singers of considerable size. The band's exemplary rhythm and blues had the audience on their feet for much of their performance and actually dancing, a rarity at outdoor rock gigs at the time. So too did The Edgar Broughton Band during their inevitable rendition of 'Out Demons Out'. Possibly one of the hairiest bands on the planet, they had shown on their third album, released the previous year, that they could display some subtlety of approach when pushed; but live they produced a relentless, wailing noise. Ten minutes into the aforementioned track, with a good-sized section of the crowd bellowing its message, Jennie turned to me and likened it to some medieval witch burning. I think she'd had enough, but we stayed for one more act –and we were glad we did.

Focus were a triumph, and this was their breakthrough gig: the entire arena stood to applaud their performance, which was a delight and a surprise in equal measure. Their melodies seemed steeped in medievalism, with the guitar borrowing more from the baroque than blues, neatly held in place by the superlative rhythm section. And while the fluid, ever-inventive, finger-shredding licks of Jan Akkerman marked him out as the star of the show, it was flautist, organist and vocalist Thijs Van Leer that made Focus something special. For the next couple of years, they were a must-see, and nobody who saw them at Reading could ever again assume that all the best contemporary rock music came solely from America or the UK.

We received The Faces loud and clear from the campsite, and by all accounts they were sensational. Jennie and I packed up early the following morning and headed home; two weeks under canvas, culminating in a couple more nights at the Reading Festival, was quite enough for a young woman still suffering bouts of morning sickness.

Adrian Moulton

The 12th (actually the 13th) National Jazz, Blues and Rock Festival, 24–26 August 1973

1973 was the first time the Festival was held over the August Bank Holiday weekend, which turned out to be a great decision. The weather was excellent, with three days of almost unbroken sunshine. 'Reading's sunny festival of pop', blazed the headline in the *Reading Chronicle* in its upbeat review after the event.

One of the main reasons for the move to the Bank Holiday weekend was that NJF head honcho Harold Pendleton thought people would be more tolerant of the noise, following numerous complaints the previous year. The stage(s), this time expanded to a triptych, were also angled differently in the hope that the sound would travel up the River Thames and away from most residents. It worked to some degree, but inevitably there were some locals whose windows and ears were still a little rattled. The quality of the sound blasting from the PA, organised by Rikki Farr (Isle of Wight Festival and Marquee Club entrepreneur), was highly praised all round, not least by *Zig Zag* magazine, which had a stall at the Festival. They reported that the site itself was 'exceptionally well organized and the music ran like clockwork'; their one criticism was the 'lack of adventure in the programming of the acts.' Looking back with the luxury of hindsight, any music fan with broader tastes would have to conclude there were some really interesting inclusions on the bill, with a smattering of excellent European groups (at the time mainly unknown in the UK), a couple of American acts and even the return of some jazz and blues artists. These included George Melly, who wowed the crowds with his mix of eccentricity and Dixieland jazz and received an 'ovation little short of amazing', according to *Melody Maker.*

Even so, for the average punter into boogie, beer and sun, some of the diverse musical styles on offer were just too much. People became impatient, which set off sporadic outbursts of can- and bottle-throwing throughout the weekend. It got seriously ugly after Sunday headliners Genesis finished their set; as *Melody Maker* reported, the trouble came when the band finished their sensational act with 'The Knife', after over-running.

The police insisted the show had to end at midnight, so the sound was totally cut off when the band left the stage, even though the lights stayed on and the crowd demanded more. With no sound, the compères could not even thank people for coming and announce that the show was over. According to Pendleton, 'After fifteen minutes one chap threw a can, then they all started pelting the stage. Some really vicious people started lobbing bottles over the backstage and they were exploding all around us in the darkness.' Most escaped serious injury, but the nearby Battle Hospital got to patch up quite a few people. Unfortunately this embryonic 'aerial liquid' entertainment evolved into a favourite pastime for many in subsequent years at the Festival, as this writer can testify: stuck in the middle of a major battle during the 1978 Festival, a half-filled can of *Watneys Party Four* hit me square on the head and almost knocked me unconscious.

Melody Maker concluded that, in addition to George Melly and Genesis, 'Some of the best crowd reactions were won by Rory Gallagher, Fumble, Lindisfarne, Alex Harvey, Status Quo, Stackridge and Jon Hiseman. Capability Brown and Commander Cody also won many new fans.' But what happened to The Faces? Ronnie Lane, who had recently left the band, was seen out in the crowd; perhaps he partly enjoyed watching his old band struggle to live up to expectations after their triumph of the previous year. The Faces were in turmoil, mainly due to the solo success of Rod Stewart and the record companies' insistence on relegating the rest of the band to be his back-up – one of the main reasons Ronnie had departed. They were sloppy and inconsistent, with many of the crowd subdued and underwhelmed and filing out early. One track from The Faces set, 'Losing You', was released on an album of selected highlights later in 1973 which also featured Rory Gallagher, Strider, Greenslade, Status Quo, Andy Bown, Lesley Duncan and Tim Hardin – all recorded on Ronnie Lane's mobile studio, the main reason for his attendance.

Another notable face spotted behind the scenes was George Harrison, who apparently roadied for George Melly – certainly one way of gaining free entry, though you would have thought he could have afforded his own ticket.

As for the Thames Valley Police, *Zig Zag* said, 'Although they did their usual ludicrous number, using ill-disguised hippies to grab miscreants for tiny amounts of dope, the police were an awful lot cooler on orders from an inspired chief.' Despite this they still managed 83 arrests, half that of 1972, according to the *Reading Chronicle*, and again the majority for possession. This included Penelope Rippon, daughter of the then Minister for the Environment, Geoffrey Rippon.

Despite the bottle and can throwing, the majority of fans and the local and national press alike deemed the Festival a major success. Let us leave the final verdict to David Lewis, writing in *Melody Maker*:

'In a summer of cancelled festivals and disappointments, the weekend at Reading came to the rescue like the proverbial US Cavalry. Everything wrong at other festivals was put right at Reading. Everybody agreed it had been the best organised and sunniest festival in memory, the only complaint was that it didn't last longer.'

Festival ticket and original sticker (unpeeled!) promoting the appearance of French band Ange in 1973

'Can anyone use a ticket to the Festival today? Something's come up and I can't make it. It's free if you want it.' We were sitting in the bar at the Ibis Club on Scours Lane throwing back pints of lager and lime, having just played the regular Sunday league football match. I was the only one who seemed interested, so the ticket was mine.

It's hard to believe now, but £4.40 for a weekend ticket was too much for me. I was on the brink of becoming a full-time student teacher, and with a wife and a six-month-old baby to support, money was tight. I'd resigned myself to missing this year's Festival, so I gleefully seized this opportunity.

I arrived on site to catch Ange's performance, having been hugely impressed by the band at the Town Hall back in April. The Festival had managed with a single stage for the previous two years, but the organisers were trying something new this year – three stages next to each other. The main stage was in the centre, flanked by two smaller ones, on which the lesser acts performed. The PA system had been massively improved, but this arrangement required two separate lighting towers and mixing consoles, obstructing the view for large parts of the crowd. The unfortunate consequence of this was that if you happened to be sitting with a good view of one of the smaller stages, you couldn't see a thing when a band came on on the other side.

It being early on Sunday, many punters took the opportunity to sleep in, shop, wash or, much to the annoyance of the police, take a dip in the Thames. Getting up close to the left-hand mini stage was easy, the crowd here sparse. Ange pulled out all the stops, but the theatricality that had seemed so intense in the Town Hall was impossible to duplicate. With giant video screens some years off, they failed to spread their strangeness beyond the first few hundred faces, and their laudable refusal to compromise language-wise meant they remained a complete mystery to the arena, despite the improved sound system. They left to polite applause from most, but got a standing ovation from the few who, like me, had pushed their way to the front.

I had a wander around the shops in the arena for half an hour until the next act, Tim Hardin, was due on the main stage. But being at a festival on your own is rather a strange business; it tends to make you feel lonely. If Status Quo or Rory Gallagher had been up next I might have stayed, but they weren't, so I didn't. There was always next year.

Adrian Moulton

The (actual) 14th National Jazz, Blues and Rock Festival, 23–25 August 1974

Following the sunny success of the previous year, hopes were high for an equally great or even better Festival in 1974. As it turned out, the weather was very mixed and, mainly due to a pretty lacklustre line-up, only 20,000 people turned up, far fewer than expected. The reviews were mostly scathing. *Melody Maker* concluded, 'Reading used to have a reputation as a spectacle, but somebody must have got their wires crossed, because a more tedious sideshow it would be very difficult to imagine.' Ouch!

The *Sounds* team were also less than impressed, although both rags agreed that Traffic were exceptional. *Sounds* reporter Pete Makowski commented, 'Undoubtedly the finest group of the festival... their set was a treat that maybe should have been saved until Sunday.' Pulling songs mainly from their recently-released album *When the Eagle Flies*, and interspersing them with old classics, they went down a storm with the punters, too. As it turned out, this was to be their last performance in England, at least until a brief reunion in 1994.

A few other acts did stand out, although of course opinions differ, depending on the scribe. Allan Jones from *Melody Maker* raved about The Sensational Alex Harvey Band, 'They were the only band [on the line-up] with the imagination and incentive to ruin your head', whereas *Sounds'* Steve Peacock 'felt like a spectator at some curious ritual that didn't really concern me' and left to nip across town to catch Toots & the Maytals instead, who happened to be playing at the Top Rank Suite. Peacock did, however, praise 10CC, and his favourite performance of all was Saturday's G.T. Moore & The Reggae Guitars. Peacock, who obviously enjoyed his reggae, gushed, 'Great stuff and exhilarating'. He added, 'A patch of dissidents in the crowd yelled "Fuck Off" at regular intervals to which G.T. wittily rejoined "Up your arse." The local mayor and mayoress, on a sightseeing tour, looked baffled!'

Compère John Peel writing in his regular column in *Sounds* highlighted Barclay James Harvest, the aforementioned Traffic, Georgie Fame, George Melly and Beckett who, he said, were 'excellent and deserved a better slot'. He appeared distracted however, reporting that he spent much of his time 'looking wistfully at the young ladies who, bra-less and plainly and rightly glorying in their sexuality, were wandering about, cat-like and lustful'. Well, it was the 70s, and he was due to get married to his partner Sheila the following Saturday.

Peel hit the nail on the head when he concluded that 'Despite the complaints that this year's bill of fare was dull, it is much more than the music anyway and the whole is greater than its parts. The strength of the festival came... from the audience.' He was one of the few journalists at the time who really seemed to understand what festivals were about. This was also the first year that he read out the football results and, luckily for him, Liverpool won. Also, this was the first time someone uttered 'John Peel is a c**t' for some reason. Both were to become annual traditions, etched into the fabric of the Festival in future years.

Perhaps it was the lack of excitement about the musical fare that prompted major outbreaks of can- and bottle-throwing; unfortunately, this new, unwanted tradition really took hold, causing multiple injuries and a busy Battle Hospital nearby. In a particularly nasty incident, an angry mob also tried to overturn a fish-and-chip van, which caused the still-lit fryers to catch fire. Perhaps they should have tried the 'peculiar cylindrical slabs of meat known as doner kebabs' reported in the *Evening Post* that made their debut elsewhere on site and must have appeared pretty exotic in 1974.

Once again police officers, some bewigged and dressed as hippies, did their best to ruin many people's weekend with their now legendary gung-ho tactics, arresting and dragging 113 poor unfortunates through the annual makeshift courts, again mostly for possession. They were even busier the following week, when they broke up the Windsor Free Festival a few miles up the M4 and forcefully evicted thousands of hippies. This led to calls from the national press for an enquiry, and a request from Roy Jenkins, then Home Secretary, for a report from the Chief Constable.

As a full-time student with a wife and baby to support, I seized any opportunity to earn a bit of cash with both hands. To make ends meet I had been working over the summer at the old Huntley, Bourne and Stevens factory on Woodley Aerodrome, and there was absolutely no chance that I would be able to afford tickets to this year's Festival at £5.50 a pop. A few days before the great event word got out that they were hiring, so down I went to the Richfield Avenue site, expecting to be a car-park supervisor or some such. Details provided, I was informed that I was now a security guard, to be paid £5 per day, and to turn up Friday morning at nine on the button. Get in!

Hard as it is to imagine in the days of Fort-Knox-style festival security, back then it was a pretty amateur affair. For a few more years at least, a kind of hippie code prevailed at these festivals. The police tended to deal with the minor criminality – thefts, drugs, minor public order stuff – and our role as security staff was simply to shepherd people about. Audiences were changing, however, and this was the year that can fights started in earnest.

For the first time, a video screen made an appearance; between bands it showed ads for the Milk Marketing Board, starring Spike Milligan. They were quite amusing the first time round, but after the fiftieth time the crowd vented their anger by pelting the screen with anything that came to hand.

Can fights were bizarre. They would start with a few cans lobbed into the air. The people who were hit would then retaliate, and within a matter of seconds, thousands would be involved, with cans filling the sky like the arrows at Agincourt. These were the days of the *Watneys Party Four* and its big brother, the *Party Seven*. Partially filled, they acted like trench mortars, spraying their contents far and wide on impact and splitting heads in the process. To make matters even more unsavoury, they were often full of piss. The medical facilities were dealing with hundreds and hundreds of cases of split scalps and concussion. Did this stop people? Did it fuck. These gruesome and socially perverted spectacles could happen a dozen times a day and last for ten minutes at a time. This behaviour blighted the Festival for many years until all drinking receptacles were banned at the end of the 80s.

My job was to check guest passes into the backstage area. I had strict instructions not to let anyone in without one, and it was a doddle, mostly. The only drawback was that I didn't get to see much of what was happening

A plan of the Reading Festival site from the official programme in 1974

on stage. Almost everyone was friendly, and I spent the days being given drinks and fags by gorgeous groupies. There were exceptions – once I was grabbed round the neck by some drunken oaf, but since I was twice his size it was no great worry. Then there was Chris Squire of Yes. I was happily checking the passes of his considerable entourage and was politely told that he would refuse to show his. There was an impasse of about a minute, when around the corner scuttled a senior Marquee fellow who informed me that it would be OK for me to let him in. Squire looked at me with utter disdain. I have thought of him as a prick ever since.

I got to see 10CC on the Friday night, who were excellent, and Kevin Coyne, who I loved on this occasion for his joyful intensity; I bought his album *Marjory Razorblade* the following week as a result. Musically, that was that; but it had been a gas, to use a very 70s phrase.

Adrian Moulton

The 15th National Jazz, Blues and Rock Festival, 22–24 August 1975

The 1975 Festival attracted many more punters than the previous year's, owing to its growing popularity, the strong line-up and another turn of events. Just down the M4, the Windsor Free Festival had started to attract thousands after its inception in 1972., Despite the violent break-up in 1974 by the police, another Free Festival was planned for the last week of August (which included the Bank Holiday weekend), but it was again halted by the cops after the arrest of the organisers, so the Windsor crowds swelled the numbers of eager festival-goers flooding into Reading. Reading Festival main man Harold Pendleton said,

> 'We hadn't bargained on the free publicity given by Berkshire and Windsor and Maidenhead Councils when they advertised on nationwide radio and in the press to prevent people going to Windsor. They urged them to go to well-organised events and they turned up here!'

As a consequence, the attendance was much higher than expected. The licence granted by the Council to the organisers allowed a maximum of 30,000, but in the end around 40–50,000 turned up. Chaos ensued.

As usual, the event in Reading polarised opinions in the local press. Still, the police were said to be impressed with the behaviour and general attitude of the vast majority of the 'youngsters' attending, regardless of overcrowding, inadequate toilet facilities, delays and bouts of heavy rain. Sixteen-year-old Fiona Wilson became a slightly reluctant celebrity when she was hauled out of the queue on Friday and told she was the millionth visitor to an NJF/Marquee festival since they began in 1961. Fiona and her friends were given free tickets for the event and an honorary membership to the Marquee Club, with free entry to all future Festivals to boot. They got the VIP treatment and the chance to meet a band, showing fine taste when they chose Hawkwind.

As it happened, Hawkwind's Robert Calvert had made a surprise return for the gig on vocals and percussion, after a spell of psychiatric treatment. In fact, this appearance marked the end of an era generally recognised as the 'classic' period of Hawkwind. The set-list for that night was mainly constructed around the album *Warrior On The Edge Of Time*, released in May of 1975, though the band inevitably ended the night with 'Silver Machine'. Brian Harrigan from the *Melody Maker* concluded, 'Midnight came and Hawkwind departed to a great response, although a goodly part of the audience seemed altogether too stunned to offer more than a desultory peace sign.' Cosmic!

Dr Feelgood played just before and blew almost everybody in earshot away with their explosive, no-nonsense attack. Brian Harrigan again:

> 'Within an hour, before the Feelgoods stamped off, the crowd had been transformed from rather cold, partially drunk windswept festival-goers into a sweaty, steaming R&B club. Charisma is too weak a word. One expected something special... but they surpassed all expectations.'

Yes headlined on Saturday and expectations were high, but they were quickly dampened as the rain set in and the start was delayed. Depending on which report you read, this 'horrifying delay of an hour and twenty minutes', as *Melody Maker's* Chris Welch put it, was purely down to continued sound problems or, alternatively, the inadequate carpeting arrangements on the stage. The band had also insisted on using their own sound engineer and allegedly blew five speakers, which caused a muddy sound and the regular loss of Jon Anderson's vocals during the set. Many were disappointed and left early.

Other acts worthy of favourable mention were Thin Lizzy, Climax Blues Band, Robin Trower and Wishbone Ash, the headliners on Sunday.

There was plenty of bad feeling about the event locally, with the *Reading Chronicle* reporting 'Three Days of Hell' for those living near the site whose streets were turned into public lavatories, with the music louder than ever and surprise fireworks late on Sunday night frightening their children. Harold Pendleton responded that 'This year's organisation has been disrupted by crowds up to 10,000 larger than expected, and I'm very unhappy because I was also let down by contractors. Behind the scenes was a disaster', he said, adding that

'Noise control is a battle we are fighting all the time, but if anyone believes that it is possible for the sound to be totally inaudible outside the site and at the same time satisfactory on site, then that is wishful thinking. We admit we have not solved this problem, but neither has Concorde. We are trying to hit a compromise.'

The *Chronicle* also reported, 'With full camp sites, festival goers were moved on to sleep wherever they could, and some found the [nearby] Cow Lane allotments quite a comfortable refuge, especially as the odd carrot or lettuce provided a free breakfast.' Mr Pendleton allegedly personally paid compensation to irate allotment holders after these incursions.

Given the myriad challenges and issues, Harold conceded that, 'Facilities must be improved next year to cope. We have international recognition now.' The events of '75 could have caused the Council to think twice about allowing the event to be staged in Reading again, so Harold was probably relieved he had already negotiated a contract for the Festival to return for at least the following two years.

The 30,000 tickets had sold out in advance, but with so many people turning up to see Yes 'on spec', the organisers were persuaded by the police to admit as many as 20,000 extra festival-goers to avoid the town having to deal with large numbers of disgruntled fans. The result was that the Festival's facilities were stretched to their limits and there was a dangerous crush at the front-stage barriers.

As the bigger acts performed later in the day, the crush got worse and worse. From this Festival until my final one in 1993 I worked as front-stage security; by 1977 I was leading one of the two front-stage teams. My abiding memory of 1975 is of hauling distressed people (mostly young women) over the barriers, and of regular announcement from the stage by both DJs and bands for people to move back. It was a miracle that no one was killed and fortunate that the barriers used in those days were only waist-height.

This was the year that the Festival cry 'Wally!' caught on in a big way and banners with the legend emblazoned on them fluttered across the arena.

Hawkwind closed proceedings on the Friday, and during a break in their set I got propositioned by an Israeli girl completely off her face on acid. Obviously taking Stacia as her mentor, she too decided to take her top off, revealing proportions like those of a prehistoric fertility carving. You remember these things!

The new boys, Dr Feelgood, born out of the pubs of Essex and London and championing a return to stripped-down, high intensity R&B, went down a storm on the Friday. There was something in the air, as Thunderclap Newman once sang.

Saturday's headliners Yes were seriously late taking to the stage and the vast crowd was becoming more and more impatient. Rumours abounded backstage that the band were unhappy about the on-stage carpeting and were refusing to go on until this problem had been sorted. We humble workers were flabbergasted.

Sadly, Lou Reed had pulled out of proceedings, making the Sunday line-up considerably less interesting. I loved Robin Trower though, who played to a mellow crowd basking in the Sunday sunshine. Wishbone Ash did their stuff to an appreciative audience, but their best days were already behind them. Down the bill on the Saturday their natural heirs, Thin Lizzy, were just getting into their stride.

Adrian Moulton

The 16th National Jazz, Blues and Rock Festival, 27–29 August 1976

Following the considerable overcrowding and problems of the previous year, the 1976 Festival was a low-key affair, but the organisers still had plenty of challenges to deal with. The Council had insisted that attendance could not exceed 30,000, despite a request for an increase in numbers by the NJF/Marquee organisation. As a result it was not possible to book many big names for the event, which meant a less attractive offering for potential ticket buyers. Advance ticket sales were several thousand down and it was feared the Festival would make an overall financial loss.

The long, hot summer of 1976 was a legendary record-breaker, and special arrangements were made to reduce the risk that thousands of punters smoking and lighting fires might turn the tinder-dry fields into an inferno. In the event, the weather broke, easing the fears of ignition, and by Sunday the grass arena was turned into 'a soggy sea of mud and rubbish', according to the *Reading Chronicle*.

The 450-strong police contingent were very busy: the drug-squad arrested around 120 people, including a couple of fraudsters with 5lbs of fake cannabis intended to rip off potential buyers. There was also a marked increase in other crimes; over 100 were reported over the weekend, including a spate of campsite thefts, thought to be an organised operation by local thieves. Police used a river launch for the first time and saved a local man from drowning on the Sunday night. Lucky chap – although he might not have thought so after being arrested for drunk and disorderly behaviour!

The programme and tickets, along with most other advertising, proclaimed the event for the first time officially as 'Reading Rock', although the local press and a smattering of printed items had already used the wording in 1975. The 1976 line-up offered progressive jazz-rock fusion with Gong, Colosseum and Brand X, the 'cosmic folk' of Nick Pickett and the popular folk-rock of the Sutherland Brothers and Quiver. However, the emphasis was shifting further towards the heavy rock of AC/DC and Ted Nugent, in keeping with the evolving demographic, now predominately young white males out to get wasted and laid.

Alcohol in copious quantities had really taken over as the main stimulant of choice for many. This fuelled the infamous 15-minute can fight that exploded during the first appearances on the Festival bill of Jamaican reggae artists on what John Peel dubbed 'Virgin Friday': all but one of the bands (openers were Stallion) were signed to the label. Peel urged the crowd to call him rude names during the now regular can fights to distract such behaviour, leading to mass chants of 'John Peel is a c**t'. In subsequent years John famously sported a T-shirt printed with the 'compliment'. Incidents of racism were also sickeningly apparent, first aimed at The Mighty Diamonds and U-Roy and then at 'Mystery guest band' Osibisa, who were greeted by dreadful and violent behaviour when they closed the Festival on Sunday night.

Friday's highlights in *Melody Maker's* report were Supercharge, John Peel favourites from Liverpool described as 'an above-average white band and amazingly funky', and headliners Gong. This was the Pierre Moerlen version of the band, which included Alan Holdsworth, 'one of Britain's finest guitarists, who held down the difficult task of interpreting Gong arrangements with great skill', gushed an impressed Chris Welch in *Melody Maker*.

On Saturday, after six weeks of glorious sunshine, the rain arrived. Pre-punk heroes Eddie and the Hot Rods blew up a storm, even in the early afternoon slot they were given, and thoroughly impressed Peel in his report for *Sounds*. *Melody Maker* was more conservative in outlook and picked out Manfred Mann's Earth Band, Rory Gallagher and most notably Phil Manzanera's 801, who also blew Peel away.

One of Sunday's most memorable performances for many was an early UK festival appearance from future Aussie heavyweights AC/DC. They impressed many, but certainly not Allan Jones of *Melody Maker*. He spluttered about their 'crass aggression', and elaborated,

'If you think the Sex Pistols are a gang of untalented jerks, then prepare yourself, with some consideration for the preservation of your frontal lobes, for an encounter with this bunch of louts. They have, you may be aware, a guitarist who presents himself on stage in a schoolboy's uniform. I should like to hang him from a convenient lamppost by the straps of his satchel.'

– and this after schoolboy Angus had dropped his shorts and flashed his 'down-unders' to the masses! There's just no pleasing some folk. As ever, it's all a matter of taste.

I was working security at the front of the stage again, and this was a much more chilled Festival than the previous one. It was hot but there was more room to move about.

Sadly, can fights, frequent and bloody, were becoming the norm. Occasional missiles were lobbed at the stage, and one or two bands had a tough time with it. That the bands on the receiving end were black acts in an otherwise all-white line-up is not mitigated by the fact that plenty of white acts also got well and truly pelted in subsequent years.

As front-stage security we were tasked with the impossible job of preventing this in an arena that was sometimes knee-deep in ammunition. Ejections were usually accompanied by cheers from the largely peaceful crowd, but of course if hundreds were pitching in, and it was dark, we had an impossible job. We usually won during daylight hours, but after dark it was hopeless.

Virgin Records' compilation of recently signed reggae artists, *The Front Line*, had made itself irresistible by retailing at a fabulous 59p. We were, as rock fans, gradually acquiring the taste, but the running order on Friday presented a challenge. With Sly & Robbie followed by U-Roy and then The Mighty Diamonds, the crowd were offered over an hour and a half of contemporary Jamaican sounds. For a significant minority of the crowd this was too much. At first, the crowd basking in the sunshine began to get up and dance, the music perfectly reflecting the warmth of the afternoon. Midway through U-Roy's set the first cans were thrown, but the worst was saved for the delightful harmonies of The Mighty Diamonds, who bravely battled on regardless. Was racism the spur for this hail of projectiles? Possibly. In any case it was a bold decision to put on three reggae acts in a row at a rock festival in the mid-70s. Racism was to rear its ugly head further, however, for the final act of the weekend.

The organisers, for reasons best known to themselves, had advertised the closing act for Sunday night as 'Mystery guest band', and rumours were rife as to who this might be. It turned out to be the magnificent Osibisa. This London-based collective of black African musicians, while not perhaps the biggest of Festival draws, were guaranteed (or so I thought) to bring any event to a joyous conclusion. Many seemed disappointed with this choice, however. Osibisa were pelted from the first number to the last, but they kept going and somehow managed to keep the happy vibes flowing. My blood began to boil as bottles and cans flew in their direction, and I have never in my life heard such overt racism as

I did that night. Front-stage security were by this time forbidden to go out into the crowd as there were so few of us, and things were getting ugly. Eventually, however, I could stand it no more and rushed out to confront a group of ten blokes who were throwing an avalanche of cans and the foulest of abuse. I must have come across like a rabid dog, and they shrank away from me as I raved, probably incoherently.

As for the rest, The Enid guaranteed their Festival place for years to come; the eccentric Robert Godfrey proved that a personality more suited to the Proms could triumph here, especially when you play 'The Dam Busters March' as your encore. You could see that AC/DC would be huge, although the press hated them. Bon Scott's good-natured Aussie banter, Malcolm Young's cap and shorts and Chuck Berry's beefed-up riffs got to the crowd in a way that only Status Quo could then manage.

As the masses drifted away, Britain's weather returned to normal. I'd finally got to see Van der Graaf Generator and generally felt it had been a good year. But every time I read about internet trolls and their like, I think of those people abusing Osibisa just because they could, and thought it was fun.

Adrian Moulton

Perhaps the Festival of 1976 is remembered for many of the wrong reasons, but it did have its memorable performances. During the period covered in this book, the foundations had been well and truly laid, and subsequent years have seen the Reading Festival evolve constantly to mirror the ever-changing musical and social landscape. The beatniks, hippies, rockers, bikers, punks and other tribes it traditionally attracted may now largely be history, but the annual August bank holiday blowout has continued to grow in size and popularity and become a kind of rite of passage for teenagers celebrating (or commiserating about) their exam results and the end of the summer.

On a personal note, I miss the annual pilgrimage to the fields of Richfield Avenue. I've had some amazing and crazy times and seen many legendary artists there since I first attended in 1979. Unfortunately, I am no longer the target generation: the last time I attended was in 2012 when, over the entire weekend, I could count the few that looked my age on the fingers of both hands, and Adrian was one of them!

The longevity of its legendary Festival means that the town of Reading continues to be known to people from across the world. Reading people should be proud of its legacy, whether or not they have ever set foot in the pungent-smelling fields between Richfield Avenue and Old Father Thames.

Rob Callaghan

Local heroes

Compiling a list of Reading's 'local legends' was always going to be difficult and influenced by somewhat subjective criteria. Should we only allow artists with a birth certificate from the Royal Berks or Battle Hospitals? In the end we decided to pick artists that have a very strong connection with Reading and managed to achieve a notable degree of critical or commercial success. However, there are also several acts we would have liked to cover in greater detail but were, sadly, unable to include due to limitations on space or because their key musical triumphs fall just outside the years covered in this book. The Moquettes and Platform Six, for example, are not listed in the following pages for that reason – their singles came out in 1964 and 1965 respectively.

Likewise, there are artists like Terry Clarke, whose main body of work is at the other end of the time period. Though he did release one single, 'Lady', on Polydor in 1972, Terry's main success came a lot later, with a fine run of albums from 1989 onwards. As an interesting aside, he was also part of a late-70s incarnation of Heron, which featured Gerald T. Moore, whose career we describe in these pages. In fact, Moore's earlier band, The Memphis Gents, could easily have merited a section themselves.

Also involved with Heron was Bill Boazman, who added guitar to their 1971 album *Twice as Nice & Half the Price*. Boazman was from a military family and had a peripatetic youth; he moved to Reading in the late 60s and was frequently to be spotted playing in the town. He later used the soubriquet Sonny Black and released several albums, the first in 1978.

As one might expect, students studying at Reading University formed several bands, perhaps the foremost during this era being Graphite. The band crop up in copious Reading gig listings in the early 70s, though unfortunately they didn't get to record an album during their lifetime. However, they managed to release a single, 'Gimme Your Number', on Beacon Records in 1972 and another, 'Come Back', under the pseudonym Sinbad in 1974. Their laid-back, prog-influenced sound can be enjoyed on a recent CD titled *Chestnut Loke*, which compiles their demo recordings and confirms they were easily the equal of many other bands of the time.

Another band that started off at the University were A.F.T., who formed from the remnants of an act called Glyder that had played the Target during their short lifespan in 1973–74. With a few personnel changes, the newly christened A.F.T. managed to secure a record deal with the venerable progressive label Charisma and released an album titled *Automatic Fine Tuning* in 1976. They also played the Reading Festival that year, but despite a very inventive sound that fused classically influenced electric guitar work with prog rock they failed to achieve much success. On a similar note, folk act Spredthick also emerged from the University, though their sole self-titled album from 1979 falls outside of our time horizon.

One mystery entity around at this time about which little information could be found were a duo called Richmond who released an album titled *Frightened* on Dart Records in 1973. The band were previously known as Shillingford Mill and apparently attended Bulmershe College in the early 70s to train as teachers, though we were unable to trace either member.

One final act very worthy of mention are Clayson and the Argonauts. Alan Clayson was a student at Bulmershe College in the early 70s and played in a folk band called Turnpike while living close to Cemetery Junction. By 1976 he had formed Clayson and the Argonauts, who received a glowing write-up in the *New Musical Express* that year. More critical success followed, and the band signed to Virgin Records, putting out a single, 'The Taster', in 1978; unfortunately their career stalled shortly after. Clayson went on to enjoy great success as a rock biographer, continued to make music with the Argonauts and still plays live with the band to this day.

Mike Oldfield

Much has been written about Mike Oldfield and his classic 1973 album *Tubular Bells,* however his early life in Reading is less well known.

Born in Battle Hospital in Reading in 1953, Mike grew up in Monks Way before moving to Western Elms Avenue alongside his musical siblings Sally and Terry. He moved schools several times, attending Highlands in Tilehurst, St Edwards at the top of Western Elms Avenue, St Josephs and Presentation College. His early life was dogged by tragic family circumstances that many have speculated led to his insularity and extreme concentration on developing his musical abilities. His musical talent was evident from the age of seven, when he began playing his father's guitar. As the 60s progressed, he was inspired by the likes of Bert Jansch and Bob Dylan. He comments in his autobiography, *Changeling*: '[At the folk clubs] I could go and see what I thought were 'proper' musicians. Sometimes I'd go with my sister and one of her best friends from school, a girl called Marianne Faithfull.' He himself began playing in these clubs at just 12 years old, joining in with older musicians on guitar. He was quickly spotted as a musical prodigy:

'When I was about 12 years old, I was offered a residency at Reading Folk Club together with a chap called John Burgess, which meant we were playing there every week. It was in the basement of the Rising Sun pub near St Mary's Butts in the centre of town. I even remember the boss's name, Sydney [sic] Lackington. We were a proper resident duo: we used to get about four pounds for the gig.'

He continues,

'I remember on one occasion, John Renbourn came to our folk club. I was so knocked out by his playing that I instantly begged, borrowed or stole his album and set myself the task of learning his instrumentals note for note... I had a solo slot at the Red Lion in Reading, and I was playing in folk clubs around the town with a musician called Chris Braclik who was Polish. Chris and I would do a lot of Irish songs and we were pretty good.'

Oldfield achieved a tremendous amount in his short time in the town, moving to Harold Wood, Essex in 1966 aged just 13. Little more needs to be said about his astounding music, career and success, in which Reading played a small but not insignificant part.

John Stannard

John Stannard is perhaps best known as part of the folk trio Tudor Lodge, whose self-titled 1971 album now fetches an astonishing £2,000. Prior to that he was a member of Reading beat group, The Mackandas.

Born in Hove, Sussex, in 1946, John moved to Woodley in 1952, later attending the Forest School in Winnersh. 'I got my first guitar at age 12 or 13,' he recalls. 'It was a cheap acoustic from Hickies and cost 7 guineas.' As the 60s progressed, John became more and more immersed in music. He recalls, 'The Olympia Ballroom was the big thing in Reading. I remember seeing The Animals, The Hollies and things like that there. I also remember seeing the Stones in the Olympia and the Town Hall.'

Before long John was inspired to join a band named The Mackandas in 1964. He remembers, 'We met in the basement of Hickies. It was *the* hangout place. You could try guitars in the basement, and we used to mooch around down there.' The Mackandas folded around 1966, after which John changed musical direction entirely. He says,

'I met Roger Strevens in Hickies. We started playing a bit and he just introduced me to Sid [Lackington] who ran the White Horse folk club. It was on the Caversham Road, opposite the Majestic Ballroom. I saw John Renbourn there and people like that.'

John and Roger decided to put together a folk duo in 1968, as John explains: 'We were trying to think of a name and we were going for an audition at a place we thought was called the Tudor Lodge so we called ourselves that. The pub was actually called the Tudor Tavern!' The Tudor Tavern was located on Friar Street; it shut its doors in the 90s. The line-up of Tudor Lodge changed shortly after, with Roger leaving and Lyndon Green and Ann Steuart joining the band.

The three-piece signed with Vertigo Records and recorded a self-titled album released in 1971, with an extremely elaborate, multi-part fold-out sleeve. The band played some festival dates that summer but soon broke up following poor album sales. Tudor Lodge have re-grouped and released music with different line-ups since then, with John and Lynne Whiteland as the mainstays. John also performed as a solo blues artist and released several albums in that style. Sadly, he passed away in 2020.

Mike Cooper

Born in 1942, Mike Cooper's voluminous discography across numerous styles has justly bought him praise the world over; not bad for a Tilehurst native.

Mike started off watching jazz bands at the Silver Bells Club (in part of the building now occupied by Marks & Spencer) in the late 1950s, before he began to play in various skiffle, blues and folk acts. This inspired him and a few friends to start their own folk clubs, beginning with the Crown Folk Club on Crown Street and moving to a club on Gun Street called The Shades. In an early example of a DIY record label, Mike and his friend Derek Hall recorded an EP of their work in Mike's kitchen on Eldon Road in 1965, entitled *Out of the Shades*.

Mike was also part of a blues band called Blues Committee that played in venues like the Latin Quarter on Bridge Street. He came across many artists who later gained fame: 'Mike Oldfield played in The Shades. He must have been 14 or something – he was very young. He was one of those horribly talented young kids. It felt a bit like "Who are you? Go away!"' Mike continues,

Mike Cooper and G.T. Moore, from the inner sleeve of Mike's 1970 album, *Do I Know You*?

'Marianne Faithfull used to come around my house. She was a convent girl and I used to give her guitar lessons. I also remember walking around Reading in 1971 and I bumped into Roxy Music, who were playing at the University. They were dressed in all their gear – they looked like the aliens had landed!'

As the 60s progressed, so did Mike's career as he signed to Pye Records and released his debut album *Oh Really?!* in 1969, which also featured Derek Hall on guitar. Multiple albums followed, including *Do I Know You?*, which had a cover photo taken at the Abbey Ruins and a picture of Mike with fellow Redingensian Gerald T. Moore on the inner gatefold. Later albums explored interesting jazz, freeform and world music territories, as Mike refused to be pigeonholed. He is still active at the time of writing, both playing live and recording with indefatigable energy.

Sally Oldfield

The oldest of the Oldfield siblings, Sally was born in Dublin in 1947. She moved to Reading with the family and spent her childhood there. By all accounts something of a prodigious talent, she excelled in ballet and classical piano. In fact, Sally was expected to have a career as a professional ballerina, but she gave it up at a young age. She attended St. Joseph's School for her teenage years, where she met Marianne Faithfull. In an interview with David Nick Ybarra from *Daeida* magazine in November 2010, Sally said they 'used to go off and play folk songs and read the Romantic poets. I played my guitar and Marianne and I would sing duets in harmony, songs like "The House of the Rising Sun" and a lot of Bob Dylan.'

Indeed, the two had played the folk clubs in Reading, as did her brother Mike. Sally went off in 1965 to study English Literature and Philosophy at Bristol University, where she continued to play the folk clubs, accompanying herself on guitar. After graduating, she made some demos as a duo with Mike at the request of Mick Jagger, who Sally knew through Marianne. This led to a deal with Transatlantic Records, and the pair recorded an album, *Children of the Sun*, in 1968, credited to The Sallyangie, a name reputedly hated by Mike. The album was mainly a showcase for Sally's voice and songwriting talents, which – though slightly raw – showed huge promise.

121

The album was not a great success, despite some positive press: *Disc & Music Echo* noted that 'As a first album it is staggeringly good – hard to imagine what their next will be like!'. Nevertheless Sally's musical career took a backseat for most of the 70s, restricted to backing vocals (she appears on *Tubular Bells*) and smaller projects. However, she had greater success from 1978 onwards, starting with the *Water Bearer* album and its single, 'Mirrors', which enjoyed chart success. This led to a whole string of successful albums through the 80s and beyond.

Arthur Brown

The 'God of Hellfire', Arthur Brown, was born in Whitby but retains a lasting association with Reading, where he studied Philosophy and Law. Brown started University in the early 60s and graduated in 1965. He appears to have been more heavily involved in music than his studies; he played in a band named Blues and Brown and made his first recording on a Reading Rag Week flexidisc, released in 1965. Credited as 'Arthur Brown with the Diamonds', he performed a dynamic cover of 'You Don't Know', a song popularised by B.B. King. The track showcases Brown's obvious star qualities and his unusual operatic vocal style.

That same year Brown joined a Fulham-based mod band called The SW5 which swiftly changed their name to The Arthur Brown Union. Having attracted a fair degree of attention, the band signed a management contract and made recordings for Polydor which appear to have been lost. The University newspaper *Shell* ran a story on Brown in its 25 June 1965 issue which noted that 'Brown had no plans to turn professional until he sang with Acker Bilk at a New Year's Eve Dance.' Amusingly the paper opined (rather disdainfully) that even if Brown achieved short-term success his long-term prospects would be poor, as his 'only qualifications would be ten years' pop-singing experience and a lower second in philosophy.' Just as well Brown never had to rely on that lower second!

When The Arthur Brown Union broke up in 1966, Brown decamped to Paris with a new band titled The Arthur Brown Set. Here he developed his dramatic stage act to complement his unique voice. Apparently becoming something of a sensation for his performances in the Parisian nightclubs, he recorded two songs for noted director

An early photograph of Arthur Brown from 1967

Roger Vadim's film *La Curée*. The band eventually changed name to The Crazy World of Arthur Brown.

He returned to the UK and maintained the band name but with an all new line-up, including the crucial addition of Reading-born keyboard player Vincent Crane. In 1967 they secured a recording contract with Track Records and released a debut single, 'Devil's Grip', in November. *Shell* featured him again on 24 November 1967 as he was booked to play their end-of-term Union Ball. Given free rein to write what he liked, Brown lambasted the 'olde worlde' atmosphere of the University, among other musings. 'Music is a man's Methuselah, Messiah and Mephistopheles. It is the massaging medium that gives the message,' he concludes nonsensically.

The band's debut album would take a while longer to appear, though when it did in the summer of 1968, replete with the pyrotechnical bombast of single 'Fire', it would sear his image into the world's consciousness so firmly that it remains fixed there to this day. His subsequent work with Kingdom Come is revered by prog-rock fans, and his Reading Festival appearance in 1971 at the zenith of that band's powers is still spoken of in reverential tones.

Marianne Faithfull

Marianne Faithfull's extraordinary life tends to overshadow her artistic accomplishments, but whatever your opinion of her, she undoubtedly burnt brightly across the 60s music scene and bestowed a sprinkle of pop glamour on the town in which she spent her formative years.

Born in Hampstead in 1946, Marianne moved to Reading aged six, when her parents separated. She comments in her autobiography,

'I went to live with my mother and grandmother in a terraced house, 12 Milman Road, the poor area of Reading... we were penniless.'

At the age of seven she started as a charity boarder (on account of her single parent family status) at St Joseph's Convent School. There she met a similar soul: 'I had one great friend, Sally Oldfield, with whom I got on well because her parents were as odd as mine.'

Marianne's interest was quickly sparked by the arts scene.

'When I was about 13, I joined the Progress Theatre, an amateur repertory theatre company in Reading. I wanted to belong because you could act and meet boys.'

As she progressed through her teenage years, she also started to be interested in folk music, singing on her own or with Sally Oldfield. She comments,

'I began doing a little bit of folk singing in coffee bars and folk clubs. There was a beatnik dive in Reading called the Shades coffee bar and another one called Café Olé. I sang a capella, "House of the Rising Sun", "Blowing in the Wind" and Joan Baez songs; "Babe I'm Gonna Leave You" and other silly things.'

By 1964, at the age of 17, Marianne had already started frequenting London's nightclubs and got swept into the music scene at a frightening pace. She became acquainted with The Rolling Stones and Andrew Loog Oldham at a party and recorded Jagger and Richards' first composition, 'As Tears Go By', which was an immediate hit in June of that year. All this occurred while Marianne was studying for her A Levels, though her pop career meant she left St. Joseph's before her final summer term ended in 1964.

The press were fascinated by Marianne, though her comments about Reading in the music papers were largely negative and created a distance between her and the town. 'You see I've led a sheltered life, what with the convent schooling and so on. Now I'm getting a chance to meet "real" people outside, if you know what I mean,' she said in an interview with *Record Mirror* in 1964.

Several singles and albums followed, though none matched the success of her debut. Her career was derailed largely by being caught up in the infamous Redlands drug bust alongside boyfriend Mick Jagger in February 1967. The issue was compounded by Michael Barrett's interview with her on the BBC programme *Personal Choice* in 1968, where she was frank about drug use. Her comments outraged the *Reading Standard's* Chris Reynolds, who wrote an 'Open Letter to Marianne' in the paper, in which he lambasted her, 'I wonder if your mother, to whom you referred as living in a tiny terraced house in Reading, felt proud of you? I didn't. Grow up, Marianne, or shut up.'

Sadly, the Redlands incident has permanently fixed an image of Marianne in the public's mind. Persistent (and largely sexist) coverage has relegated her to be the butt of numerous boorish jokes; in contrast, The Rolling Stones escaped the incident with their reputation intact. Her later life involved serious drug addiction, homelessness and anorexia, though musical triumphs like the *Broken English* LP from 1979 reveal a talent undimmed by her travails.

The Soul Trinity

Reading wholeheartedly embraced the soul and R&B scene in the 60s, with top artists from the UK and America gracing the stages at the Olympia and Majestic, to the delight of the town's mods. There were a number of local bands playing in this style, with The Memphis Gents, The Amboy Dukes and The Soul Trinity the best-known.

The Soul Trinity were a particularly interesting outfit as, like chart toppers The Equals and The Foundations, they had both black and white musicians. The black members were Kelvin Bullen (guitar), brother Hugh Bullen (bass) and vocalist Davy Gaynor, and the white musicians were Denny Ilett (trumpet), Chris Cope (drums) and, at various times, Geoff Hawkins or Allan Cooke on sax.

The Machine Gun Company (with Mike Cooper second from left) in 1972

Kelvin and Hugh Bullen arrived in Reading from Trinidad and Tobago in 1959 and soon realized that music was their calling. They joined The Soul Trinity while still at school; Kelvin was 17 and Hugh just 15. They cut their teeth in the town's clubs and church halls before being snapped up by the Ricky-Tick organisation, which catapulted them into playing the top London clubs such as the Flamingo and the Marquee, as well as further afield. They supported Cream at the Newbury Corn Exchange in September 1966, but probably their greatest moment was supporting Jimi Hendrix at the Colchester Corn Exchange in February 1967. A video clip of them at this gig shows them performing a lively version of the classic 'Barefootin'', and it's a shame the band never released any records given their obvious qualities.

During 1968 the band split, and the talented Bullen brothers joined soul band Joe E. Young & The Toniks. Following that band's demise, Kelvin worked mainly overseas, continuing his lengthy musical career in Italy, the USA and Switzerland as a session guitarist, arranger, writer and producer with numerous artists. Hugh initially played with Herbie Goins & The Nightimers before he, too, drifted to Italy, where he appeared with a number of artists. He returned to the UK for a short period, playing in a later version of funk band Gonzalez, before returning to Italy, where he lived until his death in November 2016.

Of the other Soul Trinity members, Denny Ilett forged an illustrious career in the jazz world, including a stint with The Temperance Seven, who were extremely popular with their renditions of the jazz and popular music of the 1920s and 30s. Geoff Hawkins played in two of Mike Cooper's bands, The Blues Committee and The Machine Gun Co., as well as a number of jazz outfits.

Andy Mackay

Much like Arthur Brown, Andy Mackay is an adoptive son of Reading, having studied at the University and retaining an association with the town ever since. Born in 1947 in Cornwall before moving with his family to London, Mackay was a classically trained woodwind player. In 1965 he started at Reading University, studying music and English literature, though he seemed to take more interest in the vibrant arts scene going on in the University at that time.

Reading was one of the few universities that offered a fine art degree at that time, so it attracted a crowd of people looking to experiment with the medium, in keeping with the mood of the decade. Mackay commented in an interview,

'The thing that gave Reading an edge was the fine art department... [It] gave the hipness that you needed in the 1960s. Art schools were still the hippest places, and so the would-be cool people would mix with Art Department people.'

Mackay played in a blues band called Nova Express, as well as being part of a performance art collective called The Sunshine Group, alongside his close friend Simon Puxley (later a publicist for Roxy Music).

The Sunshine Group organised happenings and produced their own magazine, often to a somewhat bemused reaction. Describing The Sunshine Group in an interview with *Shell* in 1967, Mackay explained, 'It's a sort of cultural co-ordination movement. We're between us interested in pushing the avant-garde elements of art.'

Mackay's music became increasingly experimental as he became influenced by John Cage and Stockhausen. He set up an entity called the New Arts Group to explore this musical terrain, and a performance at Winchester College in 1967 brought him into the orbit of a student there by the name of Brian Eno. Mackay continued to pursue avant-garde music in all its forms, and the association with Eno eventually led to the formation of Roxy Music when the pair joined up with Bryan Ferry in 1970.

As an interesting sidebar, another of the group of Reading art students in Mackay's circle was Polly Eltes who, alongside Anne Bean and several other students at the University Fine Art department, would form a performance-art group called Moodies who were active from 1971–1974. With their outrageous attire, theatricality, and integration of art and rock music, they shared many traits with Roxy Music and even attracted the attention of Malcolm McLaren, who was interested in managing them.

Mackay's career with the stellar Roxy Music needs no further comment; the band produced some of the most memorable music of the 70s and 80s and achieved both critical and commercial success. Without his experiences at Reading, Mackay might have taken a very different path, which he acknowledged when he received an 'Alumnus of the Year' award from the University in 2014: 'I learned to be cool at Reading.'

Gerald T. Moore

Gerald T. Moore may not be a household name, but he did much to popularise reggae music in the UK, and his work with folk-rock band Heron resulted in two highly acclaimed and collectable albums.

Born Gerald Thomas Moore in Reading in 1949, he attended Ashmead School in Whitley and played in various bands from the age of 14 onwards, which culminated in joining The Memphis Gents, a brass-infused soul band, in 1966. They were very well regarded in Reading and attracted a considerable mod following, though sadly they didn't make the leap to a recording contract.

Moore moved to art school in Maidenhead which presaged a complete musical change. He contributed a wistful folk song, 'I Wouldn't Mind', to a compilation called *Firepoint* on the Spark label in 1969. This compilation also featured fellow Redingensian Mike Cooper, whose records Moore later guested on. There in Maidenhead he met up with Roy Apps and Tony Pook at the Dolphin, a folk club in the town. Augmented by additional players, they formed the folk band Heron, with Moore providing vocals and guitar as well as various

National Hot House in Cooper's Wine Bar, Reading, late 60s

other stringed instruments. Cooper recommended them to producer Peter Eden, who helped them secure a deal with Dawn Records.

Heron's debut album was released on Dawn in 1970 and recorded outdoors on a farm in the village of Appleford (then Berkshire, now Oxfordshire, after the redrawing of county lines) with birdsong and various noises of nature audible in the background. Moore wrote several of the songs, as he did for their follow-up *Twice As Nice & Half the Price*, released in 1971; the title referred to the fact that this was a sprawling double-album set. A single, 'Bye & Bye', written by Moore, was also sandwiched in between the albums. It made Tony Blackburn's 'Record of the Week', but poor promotion meant it sank without trace.

Legend has it that Moore left Heron in 1972 after turning up to a high-profile gig and insisting on playing penny whistle rather than lead guitar. The band broke up soon after anyhow. Peter Eden had made a name for himself after discovering Donovan, and he helpfully retained an association with Moore post-Heron. A solo single,

'Song of America', was released in 1972 on Jonathan King's UK record label and further recordings made with Eden, although none saw contemporary release.

Eden had noted Moore's love of reggae and suggested he start a band in that genre. Thus in 1973 Moore formed G.T. Moore & The Reggae Guitars. The band quickly gained a considerable fanbase and released their self-titled debut album the following year on Charisma Records. Notably, the album included a reggae version of Dylan's 'Knockin' on Heaven's Door' as well as a reworking of Moore's 'Bye & Bye'.

A performance at the Reading Festival in 1974 went down well, with *Sounds* reporter Steve Peacock calling it, 'Great stuff and exhilarating', in his review. A further album followed in 1975 titled *Reggae Blue*, also on the Charisma label. Moore also started working with his girlfriend, Iranian singer Shusha Guppy, and spent time in Iran exploring the country's musical traditions.

The Reggae Guitars broke up in 1977, after which Moore did session work and later released many records in a reggae style. His music is a fascinating mix of material across several genres, and he is deserving of far more than just a footnote in UK musical history.

The Amboy Dukes

During the mid-to-late 60s, The Amboy Dukes were without doubt the best known and most successful of the town's home-grown bands, following in the footsteps of The Moquettes and Platform Six, both of whom had managed major label record releases.

The Amboy Dukes evolved out of another local outfit, The Villans, who included Dave Kislingbury (vocals, trumpet) and Trevor Lock (guitar). They honed their skills playing at dances in the many youth clubs, village halls and works canteens around the town, performing covers of hits of the day with a leaning towards soul and R&B numbers.

Kislingbury and Lock were joined in The Amboy Dukes by Mick Lambden (trumpet), Mick Jerome (drums), Art Claridge (bass), Rod Lee (trumpet), Ken McColm (tenor sax) and George Hall (baritone sax). Apart from Lee, who came from Leicester, the remainder were all Reading boys.

The Amboy Dukes took their name from the title of a 1947 Irving Shulman novel about a Brooklyn street gang. Of course the name was later also used by guitarist Ted Nugent for his band, but the Reading boys were there first! Their repertoire included soul and ska material, and they consequently developed a huge mod following. The band helped out Geno Washington with transportation to a gig at the Majestic one night, and in return he fixed up an audition for them with the Rik Gunnell Agency (the biggest soul and R&B agency in London) to take place at the famous Flamingo nightclub. The agency signed them up, and soon they were playing the big clubs in London and numerous gigs up and down the country.

Their link with the DJ at the Flamingo gave them knowledge of US soul records not released in the UK, and many of these became part of their set-list. They also signed a record contract with Polydor that lead to the release of six singles. The first was 'Turn Back To Me', released in February 1967, with the B side a Kislingbury and Lock composition titled 'I'll Never Complain About You'.

The band underwent numerous line-up changes over their short life. In 1967 they released their best-known single, 'High Life In Whitley Wood', a crazed ska tune which memorably mentions the Whitley bypass and gives a shout-out to the 'Caversham Kids'. Before the band called it a day, Polydor encouraged them to record singles in a more pop style, which yielded covers of 'Judy In Disguise' and 'Simon Says'. Sadly, neither gave them the chart success the band and their associates had been hoping for. Apparently, tracks were recorded for a demo album, but the band split in 1968 before there was a chance to release it.

Record shop memories

When our own Adrian Moulton was invited onto Tony Blackburn's show to discuss the vinyl revival, the great man obviously sensed his nervousness and threw him an easy question for starters. 'So, Adrian, what was the first record you ever bought?' They were up and running. You see, everyone over the age of 40 knows the answer to that question: it's burnt into the memory, tattooed on the brain – the day you gave proof of your commitment to the world fellowship of music lovers. Before your teenage self knew it, you had a collection that would be reflected in your choice of clothes, your hairstyle and even your mode of transport. Of course you remember the first record you ever bought!

On any Saturday morning, only a generation or so ago, record shops exerted the gravitational pull of a planet on teenagers eager to belong to whatever branch of British popular culture had them ensnared. The rise of the high street record shop mirrored the power and the glory of that culture. Thirty years ago, a typical high street like Reading's would boast several specialist recorded music retailers, with HMV, Virgin and Our Price the dominant players. National chains such as Boots, WH Smith and Woolworths also boasted sizeable record departments. Ten years earlier the players included department stores such as the Co-op in West Street and Debenhams (formerly Wellsteads) on Broad Street, as well as electrical goods stockists like Rumbelows on Friar Street, along with Hickies and Broadmeads, both musical instrument retailers. Even the occasional menswear shops gave it a go during the 60s. Throw the odd independent specialist into the mix, and it will be clear that the punter was spoiled for choice.

Record shops became the coolest of places to hang out; places where you could flaunt your pop-cultural identity, make friends with like-minded souls, flirt and check out the latest releases. The best had listening booths, where you could while away a Saturday morning impressing the opposite sex with your impeccable taste in music. This could backfire: local record dealer Clive Taylor remembers being thrown out of Hickies by an irate, elderly piano saleswoman for his rowdy percussive accompaniment to Jimi Hendrix's 'Purple Haze'.

For most, buying records, and specifically buying chart singles on a Saturday morning in Woolworths on Broad Street, was always going

to be just a teenage thing. For others, it became a lifetime commitment. Co-author Mike is one such person. Saturday mornings for him in the late 60s revolved around catching the bus into Reading with a couple of mates specifically to do the rounds of those shops. The Co-op offered surplus singles at two shillings each, often by obscure acts who had failed to chart and were not widely known, except to those who had done their homework. Hello Mike!

Apparently Hickies often had a bargain box of albums priced at one pound. Mike's girlfriend offered to buy him one and he agonised over his choice to such an extent that he still clearly remembers 50 years later the one he chose and the one he rejected, neatly illustrating the passion (or, perhaps, obsession) of the collector. For the 'record', he chose an album by Junior's Eyes and rejected one by Arcadium. Serious record collectors will feel his pain!

On to Wellsteads, where his mate may have let him slip a free album into his shopping, and then Boots, to see if their sale was still on. And there was still Smiths, Woolworths and Harlequin to go. Second-hand vinyl could be had from Cyril's Second-Hand Shop on the Oxford Road at a pound a shot. Happy days.

Finally, to answer the question posed by Tony Blackburn, the first record Adrian bought, aged twelve, was 'You Really Got Me' by The Kinks, purchased from Woolworths in Broad Street in the autumn of 1964 with a ten-shilling note a visiting uncle had generously given him. Cost: 6/8d. If it had been a less cool record he'd have told him. Probably.

Postscript

Having witnessed unprecedented growth since the 1970s, Reading is a restless, vigorous place to live. The arrival of Crossrail, coupled with the massive redevelopment of Reading Station, will only help to fuel the rise of the borough as an economic hotspot, but this growth is accompanied by the fear that it might become little more than a dormitory town. Returnees who left in the 70s might find the place virtually unrecognisable.

And, of course, the music has changed, and not just in style. This book covers the time when rock music was king, the authors having been born into a time when jazz in all its forms held sway. We grew up watching this new, wild sound create an identity and then morph into myriad styles. Rock is no longer the dominant force in popular music, but it has certainly not faded into the background.

Many of the popular music venues in the town no longer exist. Long gone are the Miller's Arms, the Wellington Arms and the Merry Maidens, the latter two turned into supermarkets. The Target and the Upper Deck have been boarded up for a decade; the Top Rank, the Majestic and the Thing-A-Me-Jig Club demolished; so, too, Bulmershe College. The University still books musical entertainments, but not on the scale that it once did.

If the 70s were dynamic, the 80s and early 90s were positively volcanic in music terms. A totally new generation of pubs, clubs and wine bars across town found that rock music pulled in the punters. The old Town Hall reverted to being a concert venue (a Motörhead gig there in 1978 possibly hastened the decision), with the acoustically excellent Hexagon taking its place. When the 3000-capacity Rivermead Leisure Centre opened at the end of the 80s, Reading finally found itself with a space that could compete with Bracknell Sports Centre. And compete it did, with appearances by artists as diverse as Massive Attack and Crosby, Stills, Nash & Young. Bigger still, the Madejski Stadium has hosted the occasional mega-star concert by the likes of Sir Elton John.

Since the early 90s, pubs as venues for live music have been in decline, the Purple Turtle being a praiseworthy exception. However, South Street Arts Centre, the Rising Sun Arts Centre, the Oakford Social Club, Sub 89 and the Global Cafe all regularly feature live music performances, as does the old Trade Union Club under the Face Bar banner. Even our old friends at 112 London Street, the After Dark, are hanging in there by the skin of their teeth, and folk music has secured a home at Watlington House.

The Reading Festival, of course, has gone from strength to strength, booking the biggest names and becoming a global brand in the process. In contrast, Readipop's annual festival on Christchurch Meadows may be a more modest affair but is all the better for it.

In terms of bands emerging from the town, Twelfth Night, a neo-progressive act who recorded a live album at the Target pub, achieved considerable popularity over a number of years in the 80s and a contract with Virgin Records. The so-called 'shoegaze' genre saw local favourites Slowdive and Chapterhouse gain album deals and critical plaudits in the early 90s. Reading seems a popular place for indie-rock bands to form, launching the careers of The Cooper Temple Clause, The Hoosiers and The Amazons, as well as the extremely talented Laura Marling, who was a student at Leighton Park School. In addition, the University can count jazz-pianist Jamie Cullum and eccentric rock act British Sea Power amongst its alumni.

Rock music once ruled Reading, as it did the whole of the UK and most of the rest of the world. A musical chameleon, it may no longer hold centre stage quite so often, but outstanding performers, their roots firmly embedded in its fertile legacy, are constantly emerging and – rest assured – will be playing somewhere in this town again soon.

Adrian Moulton
Mike Warth
Austin Matthews
Completed during lockdown, June 2020

Further reading

Michael Bracewell, *Roxy: The band that invented an era*,
Faber & Faber, 2007

Mike Oldfield, *Changeling*, Virgin Books, 2007

Mark Hodkinson, *As Years Go By: Marianne Faithfull*,
Omnibus Press, 2011

Marianne Faithfull with David Dalton, *Faithfull*,
Michael Joseph, 1994

J.P. Bean, *Singing From The Floor: A history of British folk clubs*,
Faber & Faber, 2014

Eddie Page, *Drum Solos and Other Crimes*, self-published, 2016

Various, *Airs & Places,* Corridor Press, 1999

Two Rivers Press has been publishing in and about Reading since 1994. Founded by the artist Peter Hay (1951–2003), the press continues to delight readers, local and further afield, with its varied list of individually designed, thought-provoking books.